Container & Small-Space Gardening for the South

CONTAINER & SMALL-SPACE GARDENING

FOR

How to Grow Flowers & Food No Matter Where You Live

THE SOUTH

Barbara W. Ellis

The University of North Carolina Press

CHAPEL HILL

Designed and set by Lindsay Starr in Quadraat and Fairplex.

Manufactured in the United States of America

Cover art: *Left: Canna* 'Phasion', abutilon, and Sutherland begonia. Photo by author. *Right:* Pots with small tree of yellow Mediterranean lemons by ChiccoDodiFC. Photo courtesy of Adobe Stock.

Page ii photo courtesy of Adobe Stock.

LIBRARY OF CONGRESS CATALOGING-IN-PUBLICATION DATA

Names: Ellis, Barbara W., author.
Title: Container & small-space gardening for the South : how to grow
    flowers & food no matter where you live / Barbara W. Ellis.
Other titles: Container and small-space gardening for the South
Description: Chapel Hill : University of North Carolina Press, [2024] |
    Includes index.
Identifiers: LCCN 2023044339 | ISBN 9781469678290 (cloth ;
    alk. paper) | ISBN 9781469678306 (ebook)
Subjects: LCSH: Container gardening—Southern States. | Small
    gardens—Southern States—Design. | BISAC: GARDENING /
    Container | GARDENING / Regional / South (AL, AR, FL, GA, KY,
    LA, MS, NC, SC, TN, VA, WV)
Classification: LCC SB418 .E45 2024 | DDC 635.9/860975—dc23/
    eng/20231113

LC record available at https://lccn.loc.gov/2023044339

Contents

Container & Small-Space Gardening for the South

INTRODUCTION
Finding Your Gardening Spark

←
Pots of hardy and tender perennials decorating the author's front steps are a microcosm of her fascination with gardening. Plants include hostas (*Hosta tokudama* 'Aureonebulosa' and 'Paradise Island'), *Heuchera* 'Plumb Pudding', variegated Japanese forest grass (*Hakonechloa macra* 'Aureola'), variegated aspidistra (*Aspidistra elatior* 'Variegata'), and rex begonia vine (*Cissus discolor*).

Gardening is equal parts art, craft, and science. Combining colors and forms are clearly artistic endeavors, while craft enters the picture when you consider techniques such as transplanting, seed starting, watering, pruning, and other plant-care tasks. Add science to the equation when you begin to delve deeper, for example when you ask questions about how compost benefits soil, plants, and soil-dwelling creatures. Entomology is a vital scientific component of gardening, too, especially because of the importance of attracting and supporting pollinators.

Botanical plant names are another factor that ties science with the art and craft of gardening. Many of the flowers and other ornamentals mentioned in this book have several different, and often confusing, common names. Common names also vary from region to region. Botanical names, most often set in italic type, are the only universally recognized proper names most plants have. For example, *Asclepias tuberosa* is butterfly weed. Botanical names are used in this book to clearly identify specific plants. Using them yourself ensures you get the plant you are looking for, whether online or at your local nursery. Food plants are the exception to that rule, since most have widely accepted common names.

But back to art, craft, and science. Science has long played a role in both my gardening and writing about gardening. However, art and craft—in the form of creativity and experimentation—is the spark that drives me when I am out digging in the dirt. I love combining plants, both in containers and in the ground. Of course, I have favorite annuals and tender perennials I grow each year, but I always make room for new plants I have never grown before. Every new growing season finds me searching out perfect spots for new plants—especially natives—whether I have grown them from seed or purchased them either locally or online. Many smaller seedlings and purchased plants end up in my container gardens for a season or two. That way, they have a better chance of getting the care they need. New plants that may or may not be hardy in my Zone 7 garden also often find themselves in containers. That way, I can move them into our cool garage for a winter or two before I decide whether they are ready to move to the garden permanently. Cold-hardy native palms and two hardy pomegranate plants are currently waiting their turn to be planted out, but I am not yet willing to let them take the next step.

Experimenting with sites where nothing seems to grow is fun, too. For my potted cacti and succulents, that means sunny spots that are too dry for most other plants. I also am always looking for plants that will grow under a notoriously shallow-rooted red maple.

The challenge of "so many plants, so little time," applies to nearly everything I do in the garden—and at my computer. One of the most difficult parts of writing this book was whittling down the plant lists to a manageable level. The book's regional focus helped the process, since I could eliminate plants and techniques that aren't suited for the Southeast. Because there are more plants out there to be discovered every season, and hybridizers are always busy, the challenge continues. Happily, that is part of the fun—and sometimes frustration—of gardening.

Commonly called chenille plant, botanically speaking this maroon-leaved plant's proper name is *Acalypha wilkesiana* 'Haleakala'. Its ground cover, golden inch plant, is *Tradescantia fluminensis* 'Aurea'.

Container and small-space gardening have something to offer everyone. Look to containers and small-space gardens if you have just moved into a new or smaller property. Think about what creative options your new place offers. Maybe a small raised bed or a big container combination is just the ticket for making a new yard feel like home. For lifelong gardeners in a new space perhaps the perfect thing is a small plot or container with a few choice plants brought from a former garden. Or maybe a recent move will let you grow tropical plants that would not have survived winters where you lived previously.

Both containers and small-space gardens also make it relatively easy to add bold color or a productive garden to nearly any spot. Even on a limited budget it is possible to get a garden going quickly. A small space means fewer plants, and you can further cut costs by harnessing your creativity and using recycled containers or materials for raised-bed surrounds.

It goes without saying that small-space and container gardens offer new gardeners the opportunity to gain experience and learn about growing things. The process of deciding just how many containers will fit in a given space, or selecting plants for a tiny plot, teaches everything from selecting a site and caring for the soil to selecting and caring for the plants themselves. Whether you choose containers, a small-space garden, or a mix of both, the small-scale focus is especially valuable because it helps keep your workload manageable. That is true whether you continue to garden in small spaces or eventually decide to create a larger garden.

Whatever direction it takes you, I hope this book fuels your enthusiasm for all things gardening. Ideally, it will spark something different in each gardener. That could mean experimenting with both new plants and old favorites, learning more about managing soil, recycling found objects to create unique containers, figuring out how to grow plants in a tiny troublesome spot, growing from seed, trying your hand at overwintering, or designing your own automatic watering system. Ultimately, I hope every individual reader finds their own jumping-off point and that each of you will be inspired to have fun, get your hands dirty, and make your garden more enjoyable than ever.

←
Flowers and showy foliage combine in this large-container grouping, also in the author's garden. *Canna* 'Phasion', with orange flowers and brilliant variegated leaves, is underplanted with an abutilon (*Abutilon* 'Orange Hot Lava') and Sutherland begonia (*Begonia sutherlandii*). The adjacent container features foliage of white-variegated abutilon 'Souvenir de Bonn'.

CHAPTER 1

MAKING A PLAN

Picking Places & Plants

← To create your own best garden vision, before collecting impulses have you trying to plant one of everything ask yourself why you want to garden. Follow that by deciding where you want to and can garden. Finally, answer the questions in this chapter to help determine what plants you most want to grow.

Vast stretches of flowers, vegetables, or herbs are not the only mark of a cherished garden. Plants can also easily reside in a single container or a tiny bed squeezed into a postage-stamp yard. Such gardens may be small, but they most certainly are mighty. Nearly any container or tiny plot can overflow with colorful plants that attract humming-birds, butterflies, and other pollinators. A cherished garden can feature a single specimen that carries special memories. Small gardens also can decorate a favorite sitting area, yield a bounty of savory vegetables or herbs, and do much more.

Containers and small-space gardens have something to offer everyone. They provide gardeners with new opportunities to test their skills. Perhaps that means trying new plants they have never grown before or tackling the challenge of planting a tough spot that doesn't seem to support anything green. For beginners, they offer a wonderful way to gain experience and learn about growing things. The process of deciding just how many containers will fit in a given space or selecting plants for a tiny plot teaches everything from selecting a site and caring for the soil to choosing and caring for the plants themselves.

Whatever your skill level, start the process of creating your own cherished garden by answering the three basic questions in this chapter.

Deciding Why You Want to Garden

No garden has enough room for every plant you have always wanted to grow. Whether you have a small garden or a large one, asking yourself why you want to garden in the first place helps you focus on the choices that matter most. It helps determine what kind of garden you want to create along with the best plants to fulfill that vision.

←

A wide range of flowers attract adult butterflies such as this spicebush swallowtail. To support their next generation, include plants that feed butterfly larvae in your garden. Some larvae feed on many different plants, while others are more discerning. Spicebush swallowtail larvae feed on laurel-family plants, including spice bush (*Lindera benzoin*) and sassafras (*Sassafras albidum*).

↑

A simple container, such as this ceramic seashell, can become a special part of a garden whether it serves as a reminder of a favorite vacation spot or memorializes a cherished friend or family member.

Is growing flowers or herbs what makes you happiest? Perhaps dressing up a deck or front porch is the answer. Maybe you most want to grow something you remember from your mother's or grandmother's garden. Or do you want to grow vegetables or herbs to use in the kitchen or share with family and friends? Thinking about the options your garden space offers and then answering the simple question "What will make me happiest?" is the key to creating your own best garden.

There also are purely practical, and very satisfying, reasons for starting a garden. Gardens can solve all manner of practical problems. Maybe plants would help hide something unsightly you can see from a porch or deck. Or perhaps you have cracked or broken concrete that needs covering. You can grow container gardens under shallow-rooted trees where it is nearly impossible to dig in the dirt. A raised bed—or containers—may be just the ticket for covering over a spot where the soil seems to mostly consist of building rubble.

Containers may be just the solution for dressing up a shady area under shallow-rooted trees such as this red maple. Here, purple-leaved elephant ears (*Colocasia* 'Black Beauty'), hosta 'Faithful Heart', and Kimberly queen fern (*Nephrolepis obliterata*) share the shade. Saucers under the containers keep the maple tree roots from reaching up into the pots.

Many of us garden simply because having our hands in the dirt is good for the soul. In this case, the reasons gardeners garden are many and varied. Maybe you want to bring a patch of nature to a new balcony, feed butterflies and other pollinators in a tiny yard, or create a pretty place to sit after a long day. A small-space or container garden is also perfect for teaching a child about gardening. Or perhaps mixing flowers and foliage feeds your creative essence. If experimenting in the kitchen is what you love, growing savory herbs, fruits, and vegetables may be the answer.

If experimenting is what appeals to you most, consider focusing on hard-to-find plants or finding a new use for an old favorite. Or try perfecting new techniques such as seed starting or winter salad gardening. If plant adoption makes you happy, concentrate on rescuing and reviving forlorn specimens from the scratch-and-dent table at your local nursery or big-box store. Or join one of the many local internet groups where gardeners share treasured plants.

Whatever your desires or situation, use what makes you happy as the starting point for creating your garden, and use the information throughout this book to discover creative ways to add plants to your life.

Deciding Where You Want to Garden

Determining where you want to have containers or a small-space garden takes thought, especially when space is limited. Depending on the situation, you may have several options or just one. If your space offers several options, site selection becomes wrapped up in your answer to the question "What you want to grow?" One spot may be ideal for the plants on your list; another, less so. Sites that offer different degrees of sun or shade, for example, will lead to two different lists of best plants for the spot. (Of course, gardening in both locations may be the ultimate answer!) If limited space means you have only one option, the next question becomes "What are the best plants for this site?" Either way, the secret to success lies in learning about the conditions your site has to offer and then choosing the plants that will thrive in those conditions. See chapter 2 for a discussion of factors to consider that affect the best spot for your garden and the best plants to choose.

Deciding What You Want to Grow

Nearly every gardener comes face-to-face with the adage "So many plants, so little time." Available space, budget, and life in general all affect what we can grow. Instead of being discouraged, though, use this as inspiration. Hone your plant selection skills by focusing on plants that best suit both your site and the vision you have for your garden. Regardless of where you turn the soil, good plant selection skills will improve your garden this year and every year thereafter.

Even a single container can add a bright spot of color along an otherwise barren sidewalk. This half-barrel planting features chartreuse-leaved ornamental sweet potato 'Margarita' along with purple petunias and orangey-pink calibrachoas, close petunia relatives.

Keep in mind that a garden center can be a dangerous place to start selecting plants for your garden. While the displays are inspiring, it is easy to be swept away. If you are selecting while you shop, take a close look at each plant you add to your basket. Beautiful blooming plants on shopping day may ultimately disappoint because they are not a good match for the conditions your garden has to offer. The best and brightest shopping-day candidates also may have a limited bloom season, need watering multiple times a day, or fry in the summertime heat. For this reason, it is best to narrow down your choices *before* you shop.

Hardworking plants are the secret to creating successful gardens—especially the smallest ones. Large gardens generally have room for flowers that bloom for only a few weeks, since space is available for many different plants that bloom in succession. Container or small-space gardens need hardworking plants—meaning plants that feature as many attributes as possible— because they can accommodate only a handful of choices. Hardworking plants not only thrive in the conditions your garden has to offer but also feature other characteristics that vary depending on your gardening goals. If colorful flowers are a primary focus, the plants on your list should produce showy flowers over a long bloom season. To further narrow the field, look for plants with especially ornamental foliage. That means bold texture, bright color, variegation, and other such qualities. Are any of those same plants heat and/or drought tolerant? Do they also support pollinators? If you can say yes to all, you are looking at a hardworking plant candidate. The plant lists in chapter 3 contain many plants that have passed this test and are suitable for the Southeast.

Foliage is as important as flowers when planning a small-space or container garden that will be colorful all season. This grouping, which will be eye-catching from spring to frost, includes several hardworking foliage plants: variegated *Canna* 'Phasion', plus lacy-leaved 'Kiwi Fern' and orange Sedona series coleus.

If you have room for only a single plant or two, try looking for one with an unusual color that stands out. For example, red zonal geraniums (*Pelargonium × hortorum*) are universally popular, but other colors—orange, burgundy, hot pink, and white—also are available. In addition to consulting the plant lists in this book, also ask friends and neighbors who garden for ideas and visit local public plantings. There also are countless ideas on the internet. When looking online, though, take care to identify where each writer is located. Garden writers in other areas of the country or the world may not have to consider a plant's tolerance of southern heat and humidity, for example.

If you are already shopping at a garden center, take time to read signs and plant labels to find out what you can expect from each plant. If you are at a well-stocked garden center, and not a big-box store, ask staff for expert advice. Top-notch garden centers also may have excellent displays that inspire.

Hardworking plants also are best for food gardens, but the criteria are different because produce is the main goal. If you have gardening friends or family in the vicinity—or a local farm stand—you'll already have tomatoes, squash, and other popular crops readily available during the height of the season. For your own garden, look instead for unusual vegetables or rarer forms of common ones that are harder to find. Striped or yellow pear heirloom tomatoes, purple or mini sweet peppers, and burgundy okra are just the tip of the iceberg. For salad gardens, instead of growing common lettuce, consider mesclun mixes, corn salad, and other hard-to-find greens.

Unusual vegetables are often a good choice for a small-space or container garden. Also look for compact selections as well as ones that feature outstanding color, such as 'Red Magic' Swiss chard.

The author's container garden attests to
the fact that the plant-obsessed among us
will never tire of adding new treasures and
experimenting with new combinations.

Cooking herbs you use most are probably the best ones to grow. A handy kitchen plot makes it easy to snip fresh-grown flavor. If you want a particular herb in quantity for preserving—basil for pesto, for example—find out if neighboring gardeners have some to share in summer. If you do have a local source, save space by growing a single plant for daily use and make room for some other, less available crop. Thai or lemon basil along with tarragon or chives are good choices, because a little goes a long way. Hard-to-find herbs, or ones that are expensive once dried, are another option.

Have Fun & Experiment

Whether you are growing flowers or food, experimenting with new plants is part of the fun of gardening. You can look for the latest new selections, but discovering the plants that thrive in your own yard is probably more valuable. While you may not love every new thing you try, you are sure to find plants every year you don't ever want to be without.

Experiment with techniques, too. Whether you are growing flowers or food plants, crop rotation is a very practical way to keep your garden producing and looking great. Vegetable gardeners have long rotated crops to maximize production and match plants to the seasonal conditions. Replacing cool-season lettuce and radishes with heat-tolerant peppers for summer is one example. Crop rotation is as valuable a technique in a container garden as it is in a vast vegetable plot. Pansies, a winter staple in gardens throughout much of the Southeast, are rotated out and replaced with more heat-tolerant flowers come summer. Underplanting is another option for any flower garden. Experiment with planting bulbs in a container or small-space garden for an extra season of color.

Don't let a small garden curb your creativity. Seek out new colors and try new plant combinations. Look for a plant that brings a favorite fragrance to your garden, or start something from seed. Grow vegetables that feature surprising color. In short, have fun and be creative!

CHAPTER 2

DIGGING IN

Know Your Site, Pick Your Pots & Plan for Care

←

When searching for the perfect site, the difference between shade and sun can be a matter of a few feet. These containers filled with coleus (*Plectranthus scutellarioides*) receive morning sun, while a few inches away a pot planted with *Heuchera* 'Plumb Pudding' and *Hosta tokudama* 'Aureonebulosa' receives the daylong shade they prefer.

Studying site conditions may not be as fun as buying plants, but it does pay dividends. Knowing the sun or shade exposure and the other conditions your site offers makes selecting plants much easier. Why? It allows you to select plants that thrive in the conditions the site offers naturally.

Matching plants to a site means you are working with the site, not fighting against it. For example, flowers that prefer part shade may survive in full sun as long as you water frequently, but they rarely thrive. Replace them with selections that love full sun, and you have plants that are easier to care for day to day. Whether you have one potential garden site or several, matching plant to site just makes sense whether you need spots for flowers, herbs, vegetables, or whatever you want to grow.

The amount of sun or shade a site receives tops the list of environmental factors affecting which plants will thrive. Other site characteristics also play a role. Use the guidelines below to evaluate your site(s) and discover what your property has to offer. Use the information you glean to help with your selections or to adjust the garden's location to better suit the plants you want to grow.

Containers set right into a garden bed offer an easy way to add an extra spot of color. Here, two pots of red-flowered tender perennials sit side by side. In the front is cigar flower or firecracker plant (*Cuphea ignea*). Cape fuchsia or phygelius (*Phygelius aequalis*) sits behind. Both attract hummingbirds.

Sun & Shade

To evaluate the amount of sun or shade a particular site receives, observe it over the course of a day, but also think how the amount changes throughout the year. In the process, note whether you will be dealing with direct sun, dappled shade, part shade, or full shade. See the "Sun & Shade Patterns" sidebar for more on these patterns.

For food gardeners, the best motto is to follow the sun. Most vegetables and sun-loving flowers need 8 hours of direct sun daily to perform at their best, but they don't necessarily need it all at once. It also doesn't have to be direct sun for the duration. A site that is sunny in the morning, lightly shaded during the hottest part of the day, then sunny toward the end of the day may offer just enough sun for good performance. While most food crops prefer full sun, some—tomatoes, for example—will produce fruit in part shade in southern gardens. Fortunately, many vegetables make great container plants. Containers can be positioned nearly anywhere you have a patch of sun: on a deck or terrace or even along the driveway.

Noting what time of day sunlight falls is important, too. A site that receives full sun in the morning and shade, even dappled shade, in the afternoon is cooler than one that receives shade in the morning and sun in the afternoon. For more specific heat

Sun & Shade Patterns

Most plants tolerate a range of exposures. The following terms are used in this book, on plant labels, and in plant descriptions on the internet to describe sun and shade preferences.

FULL SUN. Sites in full sun receive 8 to 10 hours of direct, uninterrupted sunlight per day during the summer months.

PART SUN. Also called partial sun, this term describes sites that receive less than 8 hours of direct sun daily. Plants recommended for part sun generally need 4 to 6 hours of direct sun for best growth, and the closer to 6 hours the better. "Full sun to part sun" indicates a plant that prefers full sun but can tolerate less.

PART SHADE. This term refers to sites that are in shade for part of the day and sun the rest of the day. Sites in part shade differ greatly depending on the duration, timing, and density of the shade. In general, plants that need part shade should receive no more than 6 hours of direct sun daily. Most do better with less and are happiest receiving sun in the morning and shade during the hottest part of the day. A spot with dappled daylong shade may also work.

DAPPLED SHADE. This term refers to a site with changing patches of sun and shade throughout the day. For example, the bright shade under a tall tree is typically referred to as dappled shade. Plants that grow naturally on the edges of woodlands and in clearings in the woods are typically plants that thrive in dappled shade.

SHADE. Also called full shade, this term refers to sites that do not receive any direct sun throughout the day. Shady sites still can offer plenty of light, but plants are protected from the direct rays of the sun by overhead foliage or even shade cast by buildings. However, few plants survive in the dense full shade under evergreen trees. A site next to the north side of a building also may not offer enough light for all but the most shade-tolerant plants. Many spring bulbs and woodland wildflowers thrive in full shade because they sprout, flower, and die back before deciduous trees above leaf out.

tolerance ratings, the American Horticultural Society's heat zone map indicates zones based on the average number of days above 86°F.

Plan for Traffic & Access

Convenience and visibility both play roles when picking the perfect site. Whenever possible, both flower and food gardeners should look for a spot away from play areas or other center-of-the-yard activity spots. A site visible from indoors or that you pass by daily is ideal, since both factors help remind you to keep up with basic maintenance. Level sites make gardening easiest, but it is possible to build terraces to create gardening space. Also, well-drained sites are best, because it is difficult to grow most plants where water stands after a rain. A raised bed or containers raised above the soil surface are options for sites that are wet periodically.

Planning for access is especially important when installing a raised bed or in-ground garden simply because these are harder to move than containers. Identify essential walkways and steps that need to be kept clear, and also allow for adequate space around sitting areas, barbecue

Double-Duty Gardens

Whether filled with flowers or food, gardens can help solve problems. Take time to look at potential sites from as many angles as possible, including from indoors. Containers or raised beds make gardening on a site with horrendous soil possible. They also can hide unsightly views such as trash cans or the back of a neighbor's shed. A grouping of containers—or even just one large pot—can keep visitors away from a hard-to-fix tripping hazard. Trellised vines or taller plants can add privacy to a sitting area, or they can be used to highlight a landscape feature or decorate a boring fence line. Perhaps you can position a container or two to enjoy from the kitchen sink or living room window. Also look for other spots where a garden would be enjoyable, such as near the sidewalk to greet visitors or next to a sitting area where you settle in for a drink at the end of the day.

←

In this street-side garden, a raised bed constructed of stacked stone creates space for growing zinnias and other plants between the sidewalk and a charming painted picket fence.

→

When searching for sites, also look for spaces to pause and enjoy the garden. This small sitting area features pavers to create easy access, plus a table and chairs to invite lingering. Lath screening behind the shrubs that surround the spot provides extra privacy.

grills, and other features. Walkways designed for single-file access should be at minimum 2 feet wide. Don't overlook maintaining access to the hose bib or essentials such as meters, where regular access is necessary.

Also keep an eye out for tripping hazards, and make sure plants and pots do not cover up steps, uneven sections of walkways, or other spots where you or your visitors may stumble. If it helps you visualize, mark out locations with flags or stakes and string. Take into account the width of the plants, not just the width of the bed. If fragrant plants are among your gardening pleasures, site them so they barely touch the edge of a walkway but do not hide it completely. That way, passersby will brush up against plants and release their fragrance.

←
Shallow tree roots and compacted soil in this narrow urban garden make digging nearly impossible. To solve the problem, this resourceful gardener grows nearly everything in containers. A brick walkway running down the center provides access.

↑
While plants crowd the walkway by midsummer, it is wide enough to allow access for watering and other maintenance. More important, there's room to enjoy the greenery.

Easy access to water makes caring for your garden simpler, which is especially helpful on busy days when you notice a plant that needs immediate attention. In a small garden, a gallon jug from the kitchen sink may suffice, but try to find a spot with access to a hose. Adding a two- or four-way splitter to your hose bib, then running a hose to the garden, eliminates the need to connect and disconnect hoses all season. If you are using a rain barrel, attach a hose that reaches the garden or makes it easy to fill a watering can.

Also think about how you will transport bulk items such as mulch or potting soil to the garden. Will wider walkways make transport easier? Is there room for a work area where you can pot plants or make compost?

For sites under shallow-rooted trees, container gardens are an option. If deer and other pests are active in your neighborhood, consider a site that is or can be fenced.

AIR CIRCULATION

A site with good air circulation makes life easier for plants, even those that thrive despite summertime heat and humidity. Good air circulation also helps reduce problems with diseases such as mildew. Inadequate air circulation can exacerbate heat buildup in a courtyard or on a south-facing site blocked by barriers such as walls or dense shrubs. Keep in mind the sun isn't the only source of heat. A sidewalk, driveway, or patio also can reflect heat and cause scorched leaves and plants that struggle to survive. To improve air circulation, remove or prune barriers such as shrubs. Also move pots or plantings out away from walls and increase spacing between plants or containers.

Wind also affects the amount of water a planting requires. Plants transpire water through their leaves, which cools leaf surfaces. Sun and wind increase the amount of water transpired, which causes soil to dry out more quickly. That leads to the need for more frequent watering. Drought-tolerant plants such as sedums and yuccas have thicker, fleshier leaves that make them better able to tolerate windy sites. While proper plant selection can help mitigate a windy site, erecting a screen, lath trellis, or perhaps trellised vines can help block wind and give plants some protection.

Containers & Raised Beds

Containers and raised beds make it easy to grow a wide range of plants on nearly any site. The following factors will help determine what type of garden works best for your site, budget, and garden dreams.

WILL IT BE PRETTY, PRODUCTIVE, OR BOTH? This distinction may affect your choices for containers or for the materials used to surround your raised beds. In a hardworking vegetable garden, where the primary goal is abundant produce, the appearance of the containers or raised-bed framing may not be of primary importance. Five-gallon buckets

mixed with black plastic pots may be just the ticket. (Black plastic pots heat up in full sun, so look for a site with some shade or paint them a lighter color to reduce heat buildup.) If a goal for that same garden is to welcome visitors to your home, you may want to step up your choices. Regular pruning, training, deadheading, and harvesting also help keep food plants more attractive.

Gardens that feature flowers and foliage tend to have fancier containers than food gardens, but that doesn't have to be the case. Consider mixing edible flowers with vegetables for a spot of color, and select containers that are more inherently ornamental. For a planting that is meant to be a showy mass of flowers and foliage, don't worry if a tight budget dictates your choices. Cascading plants around the edges of the container or raised bed will hide or at least soften the appearance of any pot or frame.

WILL IT BE PERMANENT, SEMIPERMANENT, OR TEMPORARY?
If you, or your garden, may be moving in a year or so, instead of investing in expensive frames or containers, consider lightweight and inexpensive alternatives.

WHAT IS YOUR BUDGET? Containers and the framing for raised beds can be expensive or they can be built from scratch for next to nothing. Even ordinary black plastic pots can be painted and made presentable. Ceramic, concrete, and fiberglass containers, plus brick or stone raised beds, are most expensive and not affordable on every budget. See the individual sections on materials below for ideas on the options available.

MANAGING WEIGHT & WIND

Considering overall weight—both the weight of containers themselves plus wet soil and plants—is vital if your garden is going to be on a balcony or deck. Weight matters even for containers on the ground if they need to be moved indoors at the end of the season. Using plastic or other very lightweight containers is the easiest way to reduce overall weight.

←
While sunflowers help make this garden pretty, other features make it very practical. Tomatoes and other vegetables thrive in sturdy, wood-framed raised beds. Weed-free gravel surrounding the beds keeps the area neat and ensures easy maintenance.

Moving a large, heavy terra-cotta, ceramic, or concrete container is a challenge, but using a plastic liner pot that fits inside the large ornamental one makes management easier. Ideally, the liner pot should fit so the top edge is just under the rim of the container and out of sight. If necessary, cut off the top edge of a black plastic pot so it doesn't show. Fill and plant the liner pot, and set it inside the ornamental one. When you need to move the container or bring the plant inside for overwintering, simply lift out the liner pot and move it separately from the container.

Adding lightweight material at the bottom of a container is another option for reducing weight. Note that this option does not really make a large cement or ceramic container actually qualify as lightweight. Packing peanuts are often recommended for reducing the weight of containers, but they mix in with soil, making it hard to reuse. A better option is a layer of empty water or soda bottles with caps in place. These can be separated from the soil and recycled at the end of the season.

There also are tools and equipment that help get large containers where they need to go. Consider using a standard hand truck or purchasing a specialty pot mover or pot lifter from a garden supply company.

Finally, while heavy containers help keep plants, especially tall ones, upright on windy sites, they can still blow over and break in bad weather. If very windy weather is predicted, consider tipping over large containers and fastening them in place. Or fasten the still-upright pots to deck railings or other supports for extra protection. Lightweight containers on a deck or balcony also benefit from being fastened in place so they don't blow away. Bungee cords are one option.

Liner pots make moving large containers easier, because plants and containers can be transferred separately. They also are useful for containers that do not, and cannot, have a drainage hole in the bottom. While this copper pot filled with wax begonias lacks a hole, a liner pot makes it easy to lift out the plants and dump excess water.

Size Matters

Remember this: over the course of a season, large containers are easier to care for than small ones. That is especially true because they do not need to be watered as often as small containers, which dry out more quickly and need watering, often daily, during the heat of the summer. Large containers may only need watering every few days because of the overall soil volume. This means plants growing in large containers generally are not subject to as much stress as those in small ones. Large containers not only dry out more slowly but also provide more room for roots to spread farther and delve deeper, yielding plants that are more drought tolerant. If large containers are not an option, consider self-watering containers or other automatic watering options. See "Caring for Your Garden" in this chapter for ideas about watering.

Although large containers need watering less often than small ones, unique small ones such as this pair of planted heads absolutely merit the extra commitment required to keep plants happy. Cramped conditions also mean the ornamental sweet potatoes (*Ipomoea batatas*) will benefit from regular pruning.

Choosing Containers

Containers are an attractive, practical way to add plants to many different situations. Most typically sit on soil, a walkway, a deck, a porch, or some other flat surface. There are many other options, however. Popular hanging baskets are useful for decorating decks, porches, and other sites. For this reason, they are typically constructed of lighter-weight materials such as plastic, wood, or fiberglass. Also consider hanging them from trees or simply setting them on a deck or other surface. There also are wooden and plastic containers that can be hung on railings, walls, or fences, plus planters that fit over the railing itself.

All kinds of tropicals and houseplants benefit from spending summertime outdoors. Plants in baskets and other lightweight containers, such as this orchid, can be hung from trees. Photo courtesy of Houston Botanic Garden.

Half-round baskets make pretty additions to deck railings or when hung against a wall or fence. They also can be fastened to walls or pushed into corners to save space. In fact, anything from milk crates lined with newspaper to recycled wooden or plastic containers can be stacked to provide height and give plants room to grow. Fasten them in place if there is any chance they could be inadvertently knocked down by passersby or if wind could blow them over. Vertical wall planters are another option for covering a wall with plants. Mounted sections of gutters with enclosed ends and drainage holes are a DIY option.

Plant stands are ideal for fitting lots of plants into limited space. This collection on a metal rack under a maple tree includes houseplants summering outdoors and perennials waiting for a spot in a garden bed.

Plant stands and racks—either purchased or homemade—offer options for growing up, not out, even in spots where space is very limited. They also are very useful for moving houseplants outdoors to spend the summer.

Containers can be used alone, but it is also fun to group them to create a larger display and make room for more plants. They also can be placed in a garden bed as a focal point to show off a handsome pot or favorite plant. In this case, set them on the soil or raise the pot by setting it on a plinth or other support.

Winter Protection

Repeated cycles of freezing and thawing can damage and destroy containers. This is especially true of terra-cotta and ceramic ones unless they are rated as frost-proof. This may not be a problem in the Deep South, but consider protecting containers anywhere temperatures routinely dip below freezing. Store them indoors in an unheated garage or shed. If you store them outdoors, either dry the soil out completely and wrap them in plastic or another covering that protects them from moisture, or empty the soil out of the pot at the end of the season.

To decorate without affecting traffic flow, consider arranging containers along the edge of a patio, walkway, or other outdoor space.

REDUCE, REUSE, RECYCLE

Catalogs and websites are filled with pictures of beautiful containers to purchase, but fashioning containers from recycled materials is a fun way to express yourself. Recycling also saves money and reuses something that would otherwise end up in a landfill. The possibilities are endless. Start the search in your own basement or garage. Look for ugly or damaged containers that could be spruced up with a quick paint job. It is also possible to repair cracks or other minor damage. Neighbors and friends may be happy to donate pots or other items to your new garden. Finally, yard sales are another great place to look for options.

Old, recycled boats and other large items make eye-catching containers. This dinghy features a drought-tolerant collection of sedums.

Found items that could be made into planters offer another creative option. The only thing that stands between a 5-gallon plastic bucket or a metal filing cabinet and a container garden is a drill to make holes that allow for drainage. Everything from old sinks or bathtubs to wheelbarrows or wagons qualifies. Other options include packing crates, plastic totes, milk crates, suitcases, buckets, and even small boats. Pot feet or other supports that keep the containers up off the ground help minimize rot. Be sure to select items that either can withstand the conditions outdoors or you don't mind watching deteriorate. For example, wicker baskets can be lined with plastic and planted, but they will rot in

←
Wooden wine boxes were used to construct this plant stand that supports petunias, grasses, and variegated ivy.

↑
White Madagascar periwinkles (*Catharanthus roseus*) are the perfect topping for this antique milking bucket.

a season or two. Whatever containers you use, be sure that holes provide adequate drainage. For larger containers (12 inches or more across), holes that are ½ to ¾ inches in diameter are suitable. Smaller holes are fine for smaller containers.

You will find more ideas for repairing, reusing, and recycling throughout this section.

Containers, pots, or planters are made from a few different materials, and you can find most conventional shapes and sizes in nearly any material. The sections below discuss the pros and cons of various materials. Once you have settled on a site and style, the decision of what to buy generally comes down to factors such as budget, weight, and longevity.

CERAMIC, TERRA-COTTA & CONCRETE

Handsome and long lasting, ceramic, terra-cotta, and concrete pots also are among the most expensive containers available—and the heaviest. To make placing larger containers easier, put them in position before filling them with potting medium. See the "Containers & Raised Beds" section earlier in this chapter for options on reducing overall weight and moving these containers and specifically on managing weight and wind. As with all containers, make sure they have a hole in the bottom to allow water to drain away.

TERRA-COTTA. Rusty brown terra-cotta pots create a beautiful backdrop for all kinds of plants. Typically unglazed, they are permeable and allow air and water to reach plant roots. Because water wicks away from the soil ball, terra-cotta pots dry out more quickly than plastic or glazed containers. This is beneficial for many

Pot Feet

Also called pot toes or pot risers, these handy items lift containers an inch or so above the surface upon which they sit. Not only does this prevent the drainage hole from being blocked and ensures good drainage but it also improves air circulation and prevents staining on decks or other surfaces. Pot feet are typically made from cement, terra-cotta, or plastic, and designs run from plain to decorative. You can also make your own with bricks, broken pavers, or pieces of wood. Provided your garden is on a hard, flat surface, putting containers on plant dollies to make them easy to move is another option.

drought-tolerant plants including cacti and succulents. On the other hand, it means more frequent watering for moisture-loving plants such as ferns. Terra-cotta also can be a good choice if you tend to overwater.

The price and quality of terra-cotta containers varies. All will break if you drop them or if they blow over in a storm. Classic Italian terra-cotta containers are more expensive than ones made in other countries, and none except the very highest-end Italian pots are frost-proof. Cycles of freezing and thawing are what causes the damage. In freezing weather, water in the medium and in the pot itself expands and freezes, which causes cracking or forces chips of clay to separate and flake or crack off. Cheap terra-cotta pots are most susceptible. DIY and recycling enthusiasts will be pleased to learn that it is possible to repair terra-cotta pots that have cracks or some flaking. Internet sites and videos recommend using joint compound, sandpapering, and sealing with paint.

CERAMIC CONTAINERS. These are made of a variety of clays that are denser and less porous than the clay used to make terra-cotta pots. (Terra-cotta pots also are made of clay. The term refers to the fired finished product.) Ceramic containers are glazed, nearly always both inside and out. The inside may be a different color than the outside. High-end, frost-proof ceramic pots are available, and these can withstand being left outdoors over winter. Less expensive ceramic containers will crack over winter or the outer layers will flake off in freezing weather, so plan to protect them.

Designing a container garden using ceramic containers is especially fun and creative, because they come in such a staggering array of colors, shapes, and sizes. Ceramic containers are suitable for all types of plants.

← Grouped concrete and ceramic containers display a colorful collection of plants. Various sedums share space with pink dwarf *Cleome*, pink summer snapdragons (*Angelonia angustifolia*), variegated ornamental sweet potatoes (*Ipomoea batatas*), and yellow-edged liriope with narrow, grassy leaves.

← Aloes (*Aloe* spp.), such as this handsome grouping growing in concrete pots, thrive in sun and dry soil. Gravel mulch protects the soil without retaining moisture around the crowns of the plants. Photo courtesy of Houston Botanic Garden.

↑ Sedums, plus a gazing ball for contrast, fill these small concrete or hypertufa planters set above the surrounding garden foliage.

Antique concrete planters are expensive but long lasting. This one features a mix of sedums and hen-and-chicks (*Sempervivum* spp.).

CONCRETE. Concrete containers bring classic beauty to a garden. While light gray is most common, a range of other earth tones also is available. Styles vary from old-school elaborate to modern. High-quality concrete containers are expensive, but they are very long lasting and can be left outdoors all year long. In areas where temperatures dip below freezing, pot feet are a good idea to ensure drainage, since water can pool in the bottom of the container and freeze. Take care to place concrete containers on a level surface, since they will break if they tip over.

Anyone interested in crafting or DIY will find a wealth of information on creating concrete containers on the internet. These containers are generally made from cement mixed with other ingredients. Portland cement mixed with sand is one option. For lighter-weight hypertufa pots, the cement is mixed with vermiculite, perlite, and/or peat. Either way, after adding water, the mix is spread over a mold and allowed to dry. For best results, read directions carefully and start small. Cement is caustic, so you will need good-quality gloves, plus safety glasses and a mask to protect against the dust. It is also possible to repair damaged concrete containers.

One downside of concrete containers is that the concrete manufacturing process produces a great deal of carbon dioxide, which contributes to global warming.

FIBERGLASS

These containers may resemble concrete, ceramic, terracotta, or wood, and they come in all manner of colors, sizes, and styles. Although fiberglass containers often are mistaken for plastic, the main ingredient in fiberglass is sand, used to make the glass fibers. These containers are long lasting and the colors do not fade. They are durable, lightweight, and relatively easy to move. They also do not

get brittle with time and exposure, are not damaged by frost or freezing temperatures, and don't need winter protection. They will crack if dropped or if they blow over, however. Also take care when moving fiberglass containers that are full of soil, since dragging or pulling on the rim can cause cracking. While fiberglass containers are not inexpensive, all these attributes make them well worth the investment.

Fiberglass containers are formed over a mold, and shoppers will find that the fiberglass is mixed with a variety of resins and other materials depending on the manufacturer. The overall weight varies depending on the additives and the thickness. Fiberstone containers are made from fiberglass mixed with stone. Fiberclay ones are fiberglass mixed with clay.

Many fiberglass containers do not have drainage holes, so you will need to drill them before planting. Use pot feet to maintain good soil drainage. Clean them, if necessary, with mild soap and a soft brush or sponge. Scratches and other damage can be repaired and repainted.

←

This rectangular fiberglass container is home to a collection of miniature hostas, wild gingers (*Asarum* spp.), barrenworts (*Epimedium* spp.), dwarf Solomon's seal (*Polygonatum humile*), and other similar-size plants.

↑

Lavender (*Lavandula angustifolia*) underplanted with fall-blooming sedum or October daphne (*Hylotelephium sieboldii*) makes a tough, hardy pairing that thrives in a repaired and repainted fiberglass container.

METAL

↓
Galvanized metal containers are available in many shapes and sizes. This pair on a metal stand are planted with pink common impatiens, red-flowered Dragon Wing series begonias, and a bit of lavender to add fragrant gray foliage to the mix. Photo by Susan Bennett.

Metal containers make fine additions to the garden, from galvanized buckets and tubs to large containers that are eye-catching and expensive. Recycled and repurposed items also are suitable. See "Reduce, Reuse, Recycle," above, for suggestions. In all cases, be sure to drill a hole or holes in the bottom of the container to ensure good drainage. Since metal containers can get very hot and burn plants, a site in partial shade or full shade is best, or use a liner pot to help protect plant roots from heat.

↑
A pair of antique black metal urns mark the front steps on an urban street. Pansies will bloom throughout mild winter weather. Once the yellow chrysanthemum finishes blooming, it can be replaced with ornamental kale or cabbage.

Fabric Pots

Called grow bags or smart pots, these are serviceable containers that last several seasons provided they are emptied and stored dry when not in use. Reusable grocery bags also can be filled with potting medium and planted. Fabric pots can be cylindrical, square, or rectangular. Size varies, too, from ones that are suitable for a single plant to others large enough for a small garden bed.

Grow bags or smart pots are useful, lightweight containers for growing vegetables and ornamentals. Their weight makes them the perfect choice for adding plants to places such as balconies or decks, where weight is an issue.

↑
This wire basket hanging on an antique front fence welcomes guests and passersby alike. It is planted with pink and orange petunias along with calibrachoas, close relatives in purple and yellow. Airy white sprays of grassleaf spurge (*Euphorbia graminea*) complete the picture.

↓
A derelict metal wagon is the perfect place to plant a charming fairy garden. Photo by Susan Bennett.

A variety of open-weave baskets made from metal make fine containers. These range from large hayrack-style baskets made from welded steel and painted or coated with black plastic to lighter-weight wire baskets. Typically, they are lined with a coir or coconut fiber liner to hold in potting medium. Or line them with plastic that has been punctured to allow water to drain. Unlike solid metal containers, these are lightweight, especially ones made from wire or for use as kitchen storage baskets. All dry out quickly and need frequent watering. Coir liners that have a second water-retaining liner are available.

PLASTIC

Lightweight plastic containers come in all sizes, colors, and styles. While a great many of them are extremely inexpensive, quality and longevity varies. Plastic gets brittle, fades, and cracks over time, but some manufacturers use additives to extend life and reduce fading and cracking. Look for the recycling triangle on the bottom of plastic pots, and you will see that #2 (high-density polyethylene) and #5 (polypropylene) are commonly used to make larger plastic containers. (Both grades can be recycled.) Rotomolded polyethylene, used to make kayaks and other items, also is used to make durable, long-lasting containers. These options make better garden investments than inexpensive plastic pots, since they are less prone to cracking and fading. Plus, larger containers reduce the need to water. Rotomolded polyethylene items of all sorts can be recycled and reused to make outstanding containers as well.

Plastic pots come in a vast array of sizes and colors. Price varies as well. Higher-end plastic pots last longer and are less likely to become faded and brittle than inexpensive ones.

Recycling and reusing all manner of plastic containers for growing plants makes sense, in part because it keeps them out of the waste stream. The large black plastic pots used to grow trees make excellent and inexpensive containers. Use them as is, or paint them to dress them up a bit. Lighter-colored paint also helps reduce heat buildup in black plastic set in full sun. Also consider drilling drainage holes in and reusing plastic 5-gallon buckets, plastic tubs, and other similar items. Milk crates and plastic baskets can be lined with cardboard, newspaper, or coir sheets, filled with potting medium, and planted. For food gardens, be sure any plastic container you purchase is rated as food grade.

↑
This garden features a collection of plants thriving in a mix of plastic pots. While most are planted, some are upturned and used as informal plinths to raise the height of smaller pots.

←
Plastic containers designed to fit over railings make it easy to add flowers to deck and porch railings. Because they can be reached without bending, plant care is simple, too.

WOOD & WOOD SUBSTITUTES

Wood is another popular container option. Wood half barrels make excellent containers. Be sure to drill drainage holes in the bottom. (Imitation plastic half barrels are available as well.) Other purchased options include formal painted planters in a variety of sizes, window boxes, planters that hang on deck railings, and raised planter boxes.

Wood planters are fairly long-lived, provided they are resealed periodically with polyurethane or varnish. The wood used to construct them affects longevity and price. Cedar is most expensive but also the longest-lasting wood commonly available. Pine is inexpensive and short-lived. Other long-lived woods include teak and redwood. Emptying out the potting medium and storing containers dry over winter also greatly extends life. Using pot feet that lift the container off the ground also reduces rot and prolongs life.

→

Wooden half whiskey barrels make long-lasting containers that are useful in a variety of situations. A site like this one under a shallow-rooted maple tree is not suitable for digging garden beds, but a half barrel makes adding a hosta under the tree a handsome alternative.

Wood boxes are fairly easy to make for experienced DIY enthusiasts. There also are lots of options for recycling other types of containers to create gardens. For example, all kinds of wood crates make fine containers, as do wooden drawers. Yet another option for containers that resemble wood are some of the wood substitutes now available. Leftover composite decking (made from wood fibers and recycled plastic) is one option.

Raised Beds

Use raised beds to create plantings anywhere in your yard, even on sites that only have rubble or concrete instead of soil. Since the sides need to reach the ground all the way around, look for a level site or determine whether leveling is an option. Another possibility is installing several smaller raised beds rather than a single large one.

Raised beds not only allow for efficient use of space but also provide improved drainage and allow soil to warm up more quickly in spring, making it ready for planting earlier in the season. Since plants are tended from the sides of the beds, walking on and compacting the soil is kept to a minimum. Finally, soil in raised beds is amended with plenty of organic matter, which results in better moisture retention.

Rectangular raised beds are most common, although they can be any shape: round, square, oval, triangular, and so on. The sides on raised beds can be as little as a few inches to several feet tall. Sides that are less than about 8 or 10 inches mean less root room for plants, unless the bed is sited on soil that plant roots can reach. Shallow raised beds tend to dry out more quickly than deeper ones, too. Stock tanks make great containers or raised beds as well. They come in several heights and just need holes drilled in the bottom.

Shrubs, such as these blueberries, can thrive in containers or raised beds, provided they have adequate room for roots. In order to prevent birds from gobbling up the crop, these plants are protected by screening.

←
This wood-framed bed in front of a natural-foods market makes growing a garden possible on top of a paved sidewalk.

↓
Stacked stone frames this raised bed, which creates the well-drained conditions sedums need to thrive.

Most vegetables—especially larger ones like tomatoes—need plenty of root room to grow well. That means higher bed sides or beds that sit on prepared soil. Taller raised beds have another advantage: if getting down on the ground to garden is difficult, consider higher sides to minimize the need to kneel on the ground or bend over to tend plants. Beds also can be constructed to accommodate wheelchair access. Timbers, stones, cement blocks, mortared bricks, or other sturdy materials can be used to create sides strong enough to sit on while weeding or tending plants.

SELECTING A SITE

As with any new site, before constructing a raised bed, study sun and shade patterns to suit the plants you want to grow. Sometimes moving a bed even slightly makes all the difference. You want a site where water drains through the bed and does not pool around roots or the bed itself. If you have no other options, consider a taller bed, and fill the bottom portion with materials that will encourage water to drain down and through to avoid swamping roots. See "Growing Mediums" later in this chapter for options.

If possible, avoid locating your raised bed near a shallow-rooted tree such as a maple (*Acer* spp.). If you don't have other options, consider installing a root barrier under the bed to discourage tree roots from taking over. A section of rubber pond liner, oriented so it blocks roots but still allows for the area under the bed to drain, will work. Cover as small a portion of the tree's roots as possible. Two or three layers of cardboard will discourage roots, but you will have to replace it after a couple of seasons. Tree roots up in the bed and competing with plants will signal it is time for replacement.

Bed size and access also affect how easy it will be to garden. Even if a 20- or 30-foot-long bed will fit in your yard, consider two or three shorter ones with access paths in between. Walking around a long bed gets tiresome very quickly, and several short ones provide preplanned shortcuts. Also, if possible, plan for access from all sides. Try to allow space between the bed and a fence, for example, and for pathways

←

Framed with recycled metal, this exuberant raised-bed garden features a creative spiraling trellis. At this end of the bed nasturtiums, zinnias, and herbs prevail. The far end is filled with tomatoes and other vegetables.

between beds to allow access to plants and enough room to carry materials such as compost where they need to go. Finally, while a width of 4 feet is a common recommendation, make your beds narrower if reaching to the center of a 4-foot-wide bed is uncomfortable for you. Also make beds narrower, if necessary, to fit the space available.

It goes without saying that you will be weeding your raised beds, but also make a weed-control plan for the pathways and areas around them. If the plan is to mow grass between beds or along the edge of your yard, measure the width of your mower's deck to make sure it will fit where you need it to go. Another option for weed control is to lay sheets of cardboard between beds and along the sides (to eliminate the need to trim) and then cover the cardboard with a thick layer of coarse mulch.

MATERIALS

A variety of materials can be used to construct raised beds. Sides made of cut stone or brick are far more expensive than ones made of wood, for example. Recycled materials such as used wood posts offer a free option. Also consider whether you want your raised bed to be a permanent installation or if you want to be able to move it periodically. Even stacked stone or brick can be moved fairly easily, while mortared walls cannot.

Finally, if rodents have been a problem in the past, consider installing a layer of hardware cloth under the sides of the raised bed. For best protection, have the hardware cloth extend above the sides of the bed or attach the edges with staples or other fasteners.

WOOD. Beds framed with untreated wood such as pine can last for a couple of seasons, while ones constructed with much more expensive rot-resistant cedar or cypress sides are much longer lasting. Consider framing with recycled, repurposed wood if you have neighbors who are remodeling or taking down a deck or shed. Composite decking or wood substitutes (made from wood fibers and recycled plastic) are another option. Whole logs also can be used to create charming raised beds. Newer pressure-treated wood is much safer than products produced a few years ago. Consider it, but do some research and read about the materials used before installing pressure treated wood. Do not use railroad ties, which contain creosote. Old tires also contain heavy metals, which can leach into the soil.

Construction Options

All the materials you need to build raised beds are available at building supply stores. If your plan is to build from wood, you will need boards cut to the desired height along with corner posts. If you are constructing beds using metal roofing or other materials, select corner posts that work with the material you have selected.

Raised-bed kits also are widely available for wood and other materials. Kits may include sides, corner posts, and everything else you need. You can also buy corners and in-line connectors in various sizes, then purchase the wood or composite wood separately to fit the corners.

STONE, BRICK, AND BLOCK. A wide variety of hardscape materials can be used to build the raised-bed sides. Look for materials to recycle to save on the cost. You, or your family and friends, may have bricks, leftover stone from another project, or other materials available. Beds with mortared sides are sturdier, but building with stacked stone or block is easier. Recycled concrete blocks are useful as well. Before buying them new, keep in mind that the concrete industry produces large amounts of carbon dioxide, which contributes to global warming.

METAL. For raised beds that will last a lifetime, consider metal. Manufactured metal raised beds are available in a wide variety of heights, sizes, shapes, and even colors. All are sleek and modern looking. There also are beds made from corrugated metal, generally with wood edging at the top as protection from sharp edges. For those who enjoy DIY and have access to surplus metal roofing or other similar materials, building your own is a good option.

Soil & Site Prep

Gardeners in urban areas or developments may need to use a spade to determine if there is any soil at all that could be improved for gardening. Fortunately, containers or raised beds are a great option for gardening on impossible-to-dig sites. Not only can they be installed over a mix of packed clay or subsoil, but containers or raised beds make it possible to garden on top of broken-up concrete, asphalt, abandoned walkways, parking areas, or driveways. Wherever you garden, always call or contact your state's "call before you dig" hotline to identify buried wires that may cross the site. On sites where there are underground wires or cables, containers or a raised-bed garden eliminate the need to dig.

If you are lucky enough to have soil on your selected site, dig up a handful and take a closer look. If it consists of packed clay, densely compacted soil, or a gravelly mix, installing a raised bed with improved soil may still be the best option. If the soil seems okay—a healthy growth of weeds is one indicator—amend it with compost or other organic matter before planting.

Far from being an inert layer of dirt that simply supports plants, soil is a wonderfully fascinating and complex ecosystem where soil particles, soil organic matter, climate factors such as freezing and thawing, and a host of insects and other soil dwellers (collectively called the microherd) interact. "Soil texture" refers to the relative proportions of sand, silt, and clay a soil contains. Loam soils contain roughly equal parts of each size particle. Sandy soils have a large component of sand, while clay soils have a predominance of clay particles. While it is difficult or nearly impossible to change the texture of a soil—by adding sand to a clay soil, for example—adding organic matter benefits any soil because it improves another characteristic of soil: its structure.

"Soil structure" refers to the way particles clump together to form aggregates, which in turn form open spaces in the soil called soil pores. Soil with good structure ideally consists of roughly half particles (sand, silt, and clay) and half pore space. Small pores hold water in the soil, while large ones allow water to drain through and they also fill with air, which encourages healthy root growth. The soil microherd helps form aggregates by consuming and eliminating organic matter, tunneling through soil, and moving organic matter around. Some creatures also bring organic matter such as leaf litter and organic mulch down from the soil surface. Not only do the compounds that result from all this activity help form aggregates, but the process also releases nutrients that plants can take up through their roots. Thus the organic gardener's adage "Feed the soil, and let the soil feed the plants." Adding organic matter to soil, not just once but on a regular basis, feeds this process. Soil structure is also the reason gardeners avoid walking on soil, because traffic crushes soil pores, affecting the amount of water and air available to roots and the microherd.

Sandy soils tend to have plenty of large pores but few small ones, so water drains away quickly. These soils burn up organic matter quickly, and adding additional organic matter every time you dig a hole is a good idea. Clay soils, on the other hand, have few large pores, so water doesn't drain though them or simply sits on the surface, so overly wet soil can cause the roots of many plants to rot. Adding organic matter helps create large pores, allowing water to drain more effectively.

Planting preparation differs based on whether you will be growing in containers, in-ground plots, or raised beds. To prepare the site for an in-ground garden, see "No-Dig Site Prep," below, for two methods. Wherever you garden, here are few basics for digging and soil care.

DON'T WORK SOIL WHEN IT'S TOO WET OR TOO DRY. Squeeze a handful in your hand: If it forms a tight ball, it's too wet. The handful should crumble easily before you dig. Clay soil forms a tighter ball than sandy soil, which may not form a ball at all when squeezed. Digging dusty-dry soil pulverizes it and destroys its structure. Water dry soil deeply before you work it.

TEST FOR TEMPERATURE. Before sowing seeds or moving transplants, use a soil thermometer or just feel your sample and use your best judgment. If the soil is frozen, wait to sow or transplant cold-tolerant plants such as peas, broccoli, and pansies. Soil should still feel cool to the touch (above 40°F) but not too warm (above 70°F). For warm-season crops such as peppers and flowers that are sown or transplanted after all danger of frost has passed, wait until the soil feels warm, at least 60°F. Soil temperatures between 65°F and 70°F are even better.

DON'T WALK ON PREPARED SOIL. This can't be said too often! Half the volume of good soil is pore space. Walking on soil compresses pores, damages soil structure, and makes the soil less hospitable to plants.

ADD ORGANIC MATTER. You can't add too much organic matter to soil. Soils high in organic matter are easy to work and have good tilth, meaning they have a loose, crumbly structure. The more organic matter a soil contains, the larger and more active its microherd is, meaning its level of biological activity. A large, active microherd speeds the breakdown of organic matter, releasing nutrients to plants. Adding compost or other organic matter to soil, and mulching with bark or chopped leaves, has an added benefit. Carbon held in soil in the form of organic matter provides long-term carbon storage and reduces your carbon footprint.

LEVEL UP

Container gardeners need to level out any sites where containers won't stand upright and are in danger of tipping. Raised beds also need a level site so the bottom edge of the frame sits against the soil surface all the way around. On severely sloping sites, consider installing a terrace or a series of terraces to create level space, which is easier to plant. Terraces also reduce runoff because rainfall has time to soak into the soil surface. If the site requires a terrace that is more than 1 or 2 feet tall, consider hiring a professional to install it or at least to review your plans. Also consult local authorities to check local building codes. You will find a wealth of building ideas, videos, and step-by-step directions for building terraces on the internet.

NO-DIG SITE PREP

You can prepare a site for an in-ground garden using one of the methods described here. If you have fairly good garden soil and want to plant immediately, remove existing vegetation, spread at least two inches of compost, other organic matter, or a mix of both over the site, then cover it with a layer of newspaper or brown packing paper, six or so sheets thick. Top that with a layer of organic mulch. When planting, dig down through the mulch and paper layers. This technique reduces the number of weeds that normally sprout on a newly prepared site.

The no-dig method, sometimes called deep mulching or lasagna gardening, is used to prepare a site in spring for fall planting or in fall for spring planting. This technique builds great growing conditions and also helps prevent weed seeds that have been lying dormant in the soil from germinating the minute you begin watering your new garden.

Start by cutting existing growth to the ground and covering the site with a thick layer of newspaper or brown packing paper, eight to ten sheets thick. You can dig up larger weeds if you like, but the paper layer smothers most of the plants growing on the site. (If woody plants or vigorous rhizomatous grasses are present, use cardboard instead of newspaper and wait longer to plant.) Top the newspaper with a 3-to-4-inch-deep layer of rotted wood chip mulch, chopped leaves, bagged compost or other organic matter, or a combination. Top off the pile with another layer of mulch. Then wait. While you wait, soil organisms move the organic matter down into the soil for you. When you plant, poke holes straight through the layers, disturbing them as little as possible.

Growing Mediums

Filling your containers or raised beds with growing medium is the final step before planting. A quick and easy way to determine how much medium you will need, regardless of the size or shape of your beds or containers, is to use one of the online sites that calculate it for you; just search for "soil volume calculator." Since the medium settles after the container or bed is filled initially, buy or mix a little bit extra and add as needed.

Bagged potting mediums are the easiest option for the average container gardener. Generally, these are soilless mixes that contain a blend of ground pine bark, peat moss, vermiculite and/or perlite, plus other ingredients. Bagged mixes are designed to ensure proper drainage along with good support for both roots and the plants they support. Some contain fertilizer, and others do not. Some also contain polymers, called hydrogels or hydrophilic polymers, that help hold water in the soil and reduce the need to water.

For gardeners who prefer to mix their own medium, a general formula starts with a mix of equal parts soil and organic matter. The soil portion can be bagged topsoil or even garden soil. For the organic matter portion, use a combination of finished compost, coir fiber, finely chopped leaves, well-rotted pine bark, or other organic matter. As you work, for every five parts soil and five parts organic matter, add one part purchased potting soil and a half part perlite to ensure good drainage. A garden cart or a large tarp helps contain the mess. When blending your own medium consider testing water retention and drainage before planting by filling a container, watering it thoroughly, then watering again to observe how fast water drains away and how long the medium stays wet.

FILLING CONTAINERS

Whether you buy bagged medium or mix your own, wet the mix before you plant, because dry mix damages roots. To pre-wet mix, either fill containers and water them thoroughly before planting or put dry mix in a large bucket or other container and add water. Generally, it is best to wet the mix the day before planting, because it takes time to thoroughly moisten all the ingredients.

Fill your containers to within a couple inches of the rim, depending on the size of the root balls of the plants you are planting. At planting time, fill in around the plants so the soil medium comes to between 1 and 2 inches of the rim. Topping the soil with mulch brings the level to about 1 inch from the rim.

FILLING RAISED BEDS

While you can fill a raised bed with bagged potting medium, other options help save money, control weeds, and create better growing conditions. Before filling the bed, cover the bottom with a thick layer of newspaper or brown packing paper, eight or more sheets thick to control weeds. You also can use a layer of cardboard. Poke holes in the paper if you think drainage will be an issue. Avoid using weed barriers that are not biodegradable, because they deteriorate over time and become difficult to remove.

If your bed is sitting on concrete or hard-packed clay, consider a layer of gravel or a slotted drainage pipe at the bottom to ensure proper drainage. You may need to drill a hole in the side of the bed to allow water to flow out. Otherwise, rainwater may simply fill up the bed.

Before filling the bed with purchased or home-blended medium, spread 4 to 8 inches of compost or other organic matter. Use the lower amount on beds that are only a foot or so tall and more on taller beds. In taller gardens, this layer can be as thick as one-third the height of the bed. In addition to compost, it also can include materials such as straw, grass clippings, small twigs, rotted pine bark mulch, and chopped leaves. If you have a compost pile, add partially decomposed compost and even kitchen scraps. Branches and logs are good additions at the bottom of taller gardens. This layer saves money on purchased medium, improves soil organic matter, and ensures good drainage.

Next, fill the bed to the top with home-blended (see the recipe above) or purchased soil medium. If you are mixing your own, combine the ingredients right in the bed as you fill. As the organic matter in the bottom layer gradually rots, it releases nutrients that plants need to grow. The decomposition process is the basis for the old adage every organic gardener knows, "Feed the soil, and let the soil feed the plants."

Once the bed is full, water it to settle the soil, then add additional soil medium if necessary. Finally, spread a layer of mulch to help retain moisture and protect the soil from rain and wind.

To keep the soil fed and plants happy, add compost periodically. Spread it as mulch or in a trench dug down the center of the bed. Your soil's microherd will distribute it throughout the bed for you. Provided your raised bed is deep enough to discourage pests, you can even bury kitchen scraps or other compostable materials such as leaves or dried-up weeds in unplanted areas. Be sure to mix kitchen scraps with the surrounding soil to make them less appealing to visiting pests that may be tempted to dig for them.

LASAGNA GARDENING AND BEYOND. There are various other methods for building soil using layers of material, including lasagna gardening and hugelkultur gardening. These methods involve spreading layers of materials that build up to the top of the bed. Start with cardboard to smother grass and discourage weeds, then add layers of the organic materials mentioned above interspersed with layers of finished compost and purchased topsoil. Add composted manure, too, among the lower layers. All these materials gradually break down as the soil feeds your plants, so plan to add more each season.

Plants & Scheduling

The basic process of starting or buying plants and getting them into the garden is similar whether you garden in the ground, in containers, or in raised beds. You will find more information on the needs of specific plants and groups of plants in chapters 3 and 4.

If you are buying transplants for your garden, avoid tall, overgrown ones in tiny pots with overcrowded roots. Also avoid plants with yellowed, sickly-looking leaves or evidence of insects such as aphids or whiteflies. Plants offered at good garden centers and nurseries generally are a better buy than ones from grocery and big-box stores because the staff is more knowledgeable about the care they require.

Local information is invaluable when planning for many key gardening activities. Gardeners in Florida or south Georgia can sow seeds or move transplants unable to tolerate cold, or even cool, soil much earlier than gardeners in Virginia, for example. Sowing and transplanting schedules are generally determined by the last spring frost date in your area or by the first fall frost date if you are scheduling fall or winter plantings. Average local winter low temperatures affect schedules, too, because they determine which plants can and cannot survive outdoors over winter.

Recommended planting seasons vary, too. While gardeners in northern parts of our region can still grow cool-season plants such as pansies, lettuce, and spinach through the winter, the main growing season typically runs from late winter/early spring through fall or early winter. During the winter months gardeners in warmer parts of the Deep South can easily grow a variety of cool-season flowers and vegetables. However, although their gardens are still growing strong, many take a break during the hottest part of summer. Hot weather makes it difficult to start seeds or establish transplants, partly because they will require frequent watering to get a good start. Instead, in the far South, gardeners often plant from mid- to late winter, grow until early summer, then start planting anew in late summer or early fall.

To determine average winter low temperatures, recommended planting schedules, and other valuable information for your own garden, consult your local agricultural extension office. Other local sources of information include experts at local garden centers, garden clubs, plant enthusiast groups, and neighbors who garden. If you look online, check websites to determine where their experts actually live and garden. Recommendations on sites written by gardeners in Great Britain or the Pacific Northwest do not necessarily translate to the Southeast!

SEEDS & TRANSPLANTS

Whether you are starting plants from seed or need to determine when to move transplants to the garden, first find the frost dates for your area. You can ask your extension agent or local gardeners. Or find them online by searching for "frost dates" and the name of your city. This search gives you a range of dates and percentage chances of when those temperatures may occur. For sowing, pick a date in the middle and adjust transplant dates according to the weather that year.

One way to save space under lights and reduce the number of pots that need care is to initially sow several seeds in each pot. Once the seedlings are large enough, transplant the healthiest ones to individual pots. Or simply cut down the unneeded ones to give the strongest plants space to develop.

Sowing and transplant dates are given on seed packets, in books, or online. To determine when to sow, you count back from the spring date: 4 to 6 or 6 to 8 weeks, for example. Use the same process for fall. Depending on what you are growing, transplant information may recommend moving plants on the spring frost date, or slightly before or slightly after it. In general, do not rush transplanting, since exposing plants to late cold snaps can damage or kill them, or be prepared to protect plants with sheets or other coverings on cold nights. See "Getting Started with Vegetables" and "Growing from Seeds" in chapter 4 for more on scheduling and seed starting/sowing.

For the first days after transplanting, shade helps protect new transplants from stress and gives them the time they need to start growing into the soil of their new home. Upturned bushel baskets are an effective way to create shade. Or spread burlap over stakes to block the hottest rays of the sun. Also take care to water new transplants regularly.

MOVING PLANTS TO THE GARDEN

Regardless of whether your last frost date has passed, seedlings and purchased greenhouse-grown plants need to be hardened off before they are ready to be moved to the garden. Set plants out for an hour or so the first day in a site protected from direct sun and wind. Gradually increase the amount of sunlight they receive while you increase the amount of time they are outdoors. If you work away from home, start on a day you will be home all day or set plants in a very protected spot and gradually move them to a less protected one.

Before you dig, check to make sure the soil is ready to work. You need to determine not only whether it is too wet or dry but also whether it is the right temperature for the plants you are going to be moving to the garden. See "Soil & Site Prep" earlier in this chapter for information on simple tests you can use to determine the best time to plant.

The planting process is fairly simple regardless of the season and the location in which you are planting. In general, rainy or overcast weather is best when planting or transplanting, because it reduces stress on the plants. To plant successfully in sunny weather, give plants temporary shade while they recover. Setting bushel baskets or plastic mesh baskets upside down over plants (prop them up slightly on one side to ensure good air circulation) or stretching burlap or shade cloth over stakes stuck in the soil are good options.

Start the planting process by gathering plants, seeds, or seedlings. Water the soil medium thoroughly a day before you plant. Otherwise, the dry soil sucks moisture out of plant roots and damages them. Also water all the plants you will be transplanting. You may want to spread a tarp to catch soil and other debris that fall during the planting process.

If you are creating combinations of flowers, arrange the plants, still in their individual pots, in the container or bed. Double-check heights and spreads on labels to make sure each plant has enough room to grow. In general, the tallest plants go in the center or toward the back of the combination. Use shorter ones nearer the front or around the edges. Look at the combination from several angles, and rearrange until you are satisfied with the result.

Working one plant at a time, dig a hole for each individual and tip it out of its pot. If there are roots crowding the surface or the bottom of the root ball, use a gardening knife or sharp-edged trowel to gently score them vertically. Vertical scoring encourages roots to grow out rather than to continue to circle the soil ball. This also is the time you can divide larger containers that contain several individual specimens.

Settle each plant into place, add any additional soil that may be necessary, and firm it around the root ball. Be sure to set plants at the same depth they were growing in their containers. If you are planting a row of plants, water each one as you go. If you are grouping several plants in a single container, water once all the plants are in place. If the soil medium settles when you water, add additional medium and reset the plants so they are still sitting at the same depth they were in their original pots. In containers and raised beds, the top of the soil medium should be about 1½ to 2 inches from top edge. Add a layer of mulch such as well-rotted bark or chopped leaves to help hold in moisture, prevent soil from being washed away during rainstorms, and make the containers more attractive. Do not pile soil medium or mulch over plant crowns and keep it from touching stems, as this leads to disease problems.

Keep a close eye on new plantings. In general, keep the soil moist, but not wet, for at least the first few days.

Caring for Your Garden

Keeping a close eye on your containers or garden beds from day to day is the best way to keep maintenance under control. Plan a daily walk-through to look for plants that need watering or other attention. Also take time to pull weeds as soon as they sprout, because that is when they are easiest to control.

WATERING

Most plants grow best in soil that is moist but not wet. To know when your plants need water, at the beginning of each season, keep an extra-close eye on them for signs of wilting. Ideally, water *before* wilting occurs, because wilting stresses plants and roots. When in doubt, stick a finger in the soil to see if the top few inches are moist or dry. Once you have gained some experience, you will be able to spot slightly drooping leaves or other early signs a plant needs watering. Changing leaf color is another sign, since color fades or turns slightly grayish when plants are stressed.

Too-dry soil, together with the stress it causes, also affects taste. Cucumbers get bitter and radishes turn hot if they don't receive enough water. On the other hand, too much water affects taste as well. Tomato plants that are watered daily, without allowing the soil to dry out between watering sessions, tend to produce blander-tasting fruit than ones that are watered less often.

The amount of watering your garden needs depends on what you are growing, whether plants are in containers or in the ground, how much rain has fallen, and a variety of other factors. For example, in-ground

Plants on the Move

If a particular plant is finished blooming or a planting doesn't live up to expectations, editing may be the answer. Don't hesitate to dig a plant that isn't thriving and try it somewhere else. Or remove and replace dead or dying plants. When warm summer temperatures arrive, replace cool-season flowers such as pansies with plants that tolerate heat. Or edit your combinations by giving plants a pruning haircut so they can regroup and continue blooming when cooler weather returns. Also dig and replace—or prune—plants that need more space or that are crowding out their neighbors.

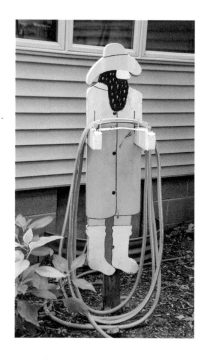

↑

Rain barrels are an excellent way to use rainfall that otherwise would be lost to the garden. Install a nozzle or hose toward the base of the barrel to make it easy to fill containers or transport rainwater where it is needed. Setting the barrel up off the ground makes the water easier to access as well.

←

To make day-to-day care easier, plan for handy access to water. Photo by Susan Bennett.

gardens generally need less water than raised beds. Plants also need less water in cool weather than they do in warm weather.

Sprinkling plants daily may be a relaxing activity, but frequent watering only wets the soil surface. That encourages roots that crowd near the surface, making plants less drought tolerant. For best results, water less often and apply enough water to wet the soil several inches down.

Water containers until water flows out the hole(s) in the bottom. If a container gets too dry, the soil may pull away from the sides. This allows water to flow down the sides of the main soil ball and out the bottom, leaving the root ball completely dry. If this happens, water several times to rewet the soil. Also loosen the soil around the edges to fill the gap between the soil and the edge of the pot to keep the water in the pot so that it can soak the main soil ball.

Consider the following techniques to make watering easier.

MAKE A PLAN. Depending on rainfall and daytime temperatures, plan on watering one, two, or three times a week—more often for container gardens. Start by installing a simple rain gauge, or maybe several of them, so you can use measured rainfall to adjust the amount of water your plants need. Most plants need about 1 inch of water a week. If you know how much rain has fallen, you can determine whether or not you need to water. Also make sure you have easy access to a hose. A nozzle with several different spray options that you can turn on and off is best. Mulch and soil organic matter also help reduce the need to water as well, since both hold moisture in the soil.

TRY LOW-TECH WATERING. Use whatever suits you to carry water, whether that is a watering can or an empty milk jug. For super-simple drip irrigation, poke two or three tiny holes in the bottom of a gallon milk jug. Set a jug next to each plant you want to water. Fill each jug with water, which will seep out right where you want it. Be sure to make small holes, since you want water to drip, not flow, out.

CONSIDER SAUCERS. In general, saucers for pots are not needed outdoors, but they can be useful. Use them to prevent water from flowing out onto a porch or other surface. While letting houseplants sit in water-filled saucers is generally not a good idea, outdoors it is not as much of a problem. Not only are plants growing more quickly, but water in the saucer can help keep the soil moist by wicking up from the bottom of the pot. If water sits in outdoor saucers, or if you are growing plants in water, sprinkle Bti granules (*Bacillus thuringiensis* ssp. *israelensis*) in the water to control mosquitoes. Bti is a safe, organic control that only targets mosquito larvae.

LOOK FOR DRY SPOTS. Keep an eye on containers and beds that may not receive the full benefit of rainfall that falls on other parts of the garden. Look for spots under house eaves or other overhead structures as well as other sites that tend to be dry. Plants growing in raised beds need watering more than those in in-ground beds, and plants in containers need even more water than those in raised beds. Depending on the size of the container and the needs of the plants in them, some may need daily or twice-daily watering. Sandy soil needs more watering than loam or clay soil.

USE SOAKER HOSES. These offer an efficient, inexpensive way to water thirsty plants in raised or in-ground beds. (Steer away from overhead sprinklers, because a large percentage of the water they deliver evaporates before it hits the soil.) The hoses slowly leak water along their length, so lay them along rows or snake them through the garden. To water, connect a hose to the end of the soaker and run it on low for several hours so there is just enough pressure for the water to reach the end of the hose.

TRY SELF-WATERING CONTAINERS. A wide variety of self-watering containers are available through gardening catalogs and on internet sites. The self-watering feature simply means all you need to do is keep the water reservoir at the bottom of the container filled. In addition to purchased self-watering containers, you also can buy kits to convert the container of your choice to self-watering. Finally, a search for "DIY self-watering containers" on the internet will yield videos and other options for making your own.

MIX IN SUPERABSORBENTS. These are a soil amendment made from crystal-like polymers that hold moisture in the soil. They are available for purchase separately or are incorporated in some packaged soil mediums. If you purchase them separately, mix the saltlike polymers into your soil medium when they are dry. When watered, they swell into jellylike clumps. Read package directions, and do not exceed recommended quantities. If added in excess, they create large lumps of jellylike material in the medium.

CONSIDER A CUSTOM-DESIGNED DRIP SYSTEM. These systems are the ultimate in efficient watering. They can be designed for you, but you can buy the component parts and design a system yourself. Drip systems can be used to water a series of individual containers as well as raised and in-ground garden beds. You also can attach them to a timer.

Self-watering containers reduce the need for daily watering. A close look at this handsome pot reveals a red gauge at the back that indicates when the internal reservoir needs filling. This container features trailing silver ponysfoot or silver nickel vine (*Dichondra argentea*) along with white Madagascar periwinkle and red New Guinea impatiens. Photo by Susan Bennett.

FEEDING

"Feed the soil, and let the soil feed the plants" means using a combined approach to feeding plants. Instead of weekly applications throughout the season, use compost as the basis for your feeding program. Mix some into the soil every time you dig a hole to plant something new, and top-dress plants by scratching compost into the soil around roots. Commercial potting mediums often contain mostly composted bark, so incorporate organic matter when you mix them to provide adequate nutrients. Supplement, as necessary, using organic fertilizers. Fortunately, an ever-widening variety is available. Most manufacturers of chemical fertilizers now offer organic options.

Flowers growing in soil that is regularly amended with compost probably will grow just fine without additional feeding. Vegetable plants tend to need more in the way of fertilizer, but too much is just as bad as too little. Plants growing in soil that is too rich, especially in nitrogen, produce lanky growth and lower yields. Don't feed during the season unless you see signs such as stunted or yellowed leaves, spindly growth, general lack of vigor, and weak stems.

Homemade compost tea is an easy way to feed both flowers and vegetables. To make a batch, put a shovel or two full of compost on a large square of burlap or in a burlap bag. Tie it shut, and drop the bag into a bucket of water. Used 5-gallon plastic buckets or plastic kitty litter containers work fine for this purpose. Let the bag soak for a few days, then dilute the resulting tea with water until it is the color of weak tea. Dump the used wet compost back in the garden or on the compost pile. Once it is diluted, use the compost tea to water containers weekly during the season or seedlings and transplants waiting to be moved to the garden. Either water the soil surface or sprinkle it on leaves to foliar feed. Also use it to feed in-ground plants as necessary. Use the same process to make manure tea. It will need to be diluted with more water, because it is stronger than compost tea.

If you prefer using purchased fertilizers, use organic ones. Natural or organic fertilizers protect earthworms and other beneficial organisms that live in and improve your soil. They also release nutrients slowly. A wide range of organic fertilizers are available, including ones in liquid and powder form. There also are bagged organic fertilizers. Be sure to read labels carefully and apply them according to package directions.

Slow-release fertilizers are available in organic as well as synthetic chemical compositions. The fertilizer is contained in a permeable shell that releases nutrients gradually. These can feed plants for as long as six months. Be aware that the outer shell may or may not be biodegradable. Those that are not contain plastic resins that break down and remain in the environment.

PRUNING & TRAINING

Basic pruning and training keeps plants looking their best. Always remove dead or diseased branches and leaves. Beyond that, however, most plants thrive whether you do a little pruning or a lot, making it easy to work around how much time you have available. Consider making time for the following tasks.

PINCHING. Pinching stem tips encourages branching and bushier growth, leading to more flowers and fruit. On young plants, pinch out stem tips between thumb and finger. Use shears to cut back older growth. Consider removing flowers at transplant time to direct the plants' energy toward roots and toward recovery from the stress of transplanting.

To cut back plants intended for overwintering at the end of the season, shape them as you would a landscape shrub. While you cut them back, look for rubbing and crossing branches to eliminate, remove branches crossing the center of the plant, and generally shape the framework so the plant remains evenly balanced.

SHAPING AND PRUNING. Use pruning shears to foster an even, symmetrical shape by cutting back or removing overly long branches or ones that stick out in the wrong direction. You also can cut back plants to make sure neighboring ones have room to grow. When cutting back branches, cut just *above* a smaller branch or leaf node that points in the direction you want new growth to go. Staking is another option for redirecting or controlling growth. Experiment with moving branches by holding them in a new position with stakes. If a combination includes vines, plan to train stem tips onto whatever supports are in place, and continue training and redirecting through the season.

DEADHEADING. Removing faded flowers lengthens bloom, because it prevents plants from setting seed. When deadheading, take a minute to see if and where new flowers are forming. You can simply snip flowers off at the base, but with many plants you get better results and more flowers if you cut just above a leaf node where a new flower or branch is forming.

CUTTING BACK. A variety of plants benefit from this technique— basically a plant haircut. Look for long branches with dead or dying leaves near the crown of the plant. While not every plant benefits,

cutting back plants that are not looking their best is worth trying.
It gives the plant a chance to rest and produce new foliage and flowers.
You can gather up stems and cut them all at once, or snip each branch
separately just above a leaf node.

TOOLS

You will need a few tools to tend a container or small-space garden but
not the arsenal needed for a full-size one. Before buying new, visit yard
sales or see if friends and family have surplus that they can share. Here
are a few that will make tending your garden easier.

BUCKETS FOR MIXING AND CARRYING. You can purchase beautiful
garden trugs, but recycled 5-gallon plastic buckets work just as well.
Use them for mixing and wetting small amounts of soil and for trans-
porting compost or mulch. Canvas bucket organizers are available for
keeping tools in order. If you need larger quantities of soil, consider
a small garden cart or even a small cement-mixing tub. Tarps also are
effective for mixing and invaluable for containing soil and other debris.

DIGGING IMPLEMENTS. For container gardens, have at least one
trowel or a gardening knife on hand. You will need a spade or a shovel
to tend raised or conventional garden beds. For moving soil medium,
especially into containers, consider a grain scoop or even a short-
handed shovel.

HAND TRUCKS AND POT LIFTERS. Even if you fill your containers after
they are in position, a hand truck or a pot lifter makes moving easier
and saves on back strain.

PRUNERS. You will want at least one implement for removing spent
flowers, harvesting fruit, cutting back plants, and other jobs. If possible,
do not settle for cheap pruners. A top-quality pair of bypass pruning
shears will last a lifetime, provided you invest in a brand that offers
replacement blades and other parts (Felco is one). Cheap tools may save

money, but they do not make garden chores easier. Quality tools also avoid supporting manufactures that produce products with planned obsolescence in mind. In addition to bypass shears, consider a pair of small pruning snips for deadheading and harvesting. If you obtain used pruners, have them sharpened by a professional or invest in a tool and do it yourself.

RAIN GAUGES. These are invaluable for keeping track of how much rain your garden actually received and determining when you need to water.

Ending the Season

End-of-season tasks include pulling up plants that have finished for the year and replacing them with cool-season flowers to bloom through the winter months. Also don't forget to take steps to protect containers that may be damaged by cycles of freezing and thawing.

If you are growing plants that are not hardy in your area and want to keep them for another season, move them indoors. For more on over-wintering, see "Annuals, Perennials & Overwintering" in chapter 3.

Winter also is a time to get ready for the next season. After the first growing season or two, plan on renewing the soil medium in containers, topping off raised beds, and adding organic matter to in-ground gardens. You do not need to replace all the soil in your containers. Replacing the top one-third to one-half is fine. Or replace enough to make it possible to work in additional compost or other organic matter. For longer-lived container residents, repot every few years. As the organic matter portion of the mix decomposes, the remaining medium becomes more dense and drainage is reduced.

FLOWERS & FOLIAGE

Selecting & Combining Plants

←
Containers are a great way to learn about combining colors, plant forms, and more. They also provide the perfect opportunity for fitting just one more plant into the garden. This combination includes *Canna* 'Phasion', the dangling bells of *Abutilon* 'Orange Hot Lava', and orange-flowered Sutherland begonia (*Begonia sutherlandii*).

The truth is abundantly apparent the moment you step into a well-stocked garden center, flip through your collection of plant catalogs, or scroll through online offerings of a favorite nursery. Growing one of everything is not a workable plan. There simply are too many plants—and too little time and space to grow them all. What's a gardener to do? How about focusing on collecting plants that not only make you happy but also are the best performers in your garden?

This chapter is focused on helping you do just that. The lists throughout are organized by site conditions, meaning plants for sun, plants for shade, and so on. Furthermore, the lists feature plants that are able to thrive in the Southeast. Pair these lists with the information you gleaned in chapter 2 regarding conditions that exist naturally on the site(s) where you want to garden. It can't be said often enough: your goal should be to match the plant to the site. Working with your site, rather than struggling against it, is as simple as filling a shady spot with plants that will thrive there. It also is about reinterpreting a combination you admire from a British garden using plants that love southeastern sun and heat. While using the lists in this chapter to match plants to your site, though, keep your eyes open for new offerings. Experimenting with new plants and combinations is part of the fun, and it will help you learn which plants grow best for you and where to put them.

Creating Combinations

If you haven't created combinations before, selecting plants can be overwhelming—so many plants, so little time, right? For best results, before you consider design features such as flower color, foliage, height, and form, remember that every plant in each combination should thrive in the same growing conditions. Focusing only on plants that need the same sun exposure and other conditions helps eliminate unsuitable choices. After that, one of the easiest methods for creating plant combinations is to design by combining thrillers, spillers, and fillers.

This garden spot features two entirely different perfect locations for plants. Conditions in the hypertufa container above provide the sun and well-drained-to-dry soil that hen-and-chicks (*Sempervivum* spp.) and sedums require. In the bed below, hostas and bee balm (*Monarda didyma*) thrive in rich soil that remains evenly moist.

Thrillers are bold plants that typically feature showy, long-lasting flowers. They also can feature eye-catching foliage—hostas or caladiums with variegated leaves, for example. Spillers are low-growing plants that spill over pot edges or out of raised beds. Ornamental sweet potatoes (*Ipomoea batatas*) or creeping Jenny (*Lysimachia nummularia*) are two examples. Fillers fill in among all the plants in the combination. They may have lots of small flowers, such as cigar flower or firecracker plant (*Cuphea ignea*), or attractive foliage, such as polka dot plant (*Hypoestes phyllostachya*). Keep in mind that, depending on its companions, the same plant can play different roles. A plant may function as a thriller in combination with smaller plants or as a filler when mixed with larger ones such as a canna or dwarf banana.

You will find ideas for combinations in the photographs throughout this book. The internet, magazines, and other publications provide an unlimited supply of ideas. While re-creating combinations from magazines or websites is one option, mixing and matching plants yourself is fun and easy. Use the techniques below to get started. And remember, you can always edit your combinations with a trowel by moving a plant to another location, by discarding something that doesn't perform well, or by adding a plant to change the combination.

↑

The thrillers, spillers, and fillers in these containers all feature foliage. Red-leaved coleus is the thriller; golden creeping Jenny (*Lysimachia nummularia* 'Aurea') is the spiller; and a second, purple-black-and-green-leaved coleus is the filler.

←

Favorite plants can inspire color combinations, but so can gardening passions. This grouping features blue-flowered agapanthus (*Agapanthus africanus*), which grows from a fleshy rhizome and is native to South Africa. North American natives surround it, including butterfly weed (*Asclepias tuberosa*) and annual coreopsis hybrid 'Jive'.

BUILD ON A FAVORITE. Select a single plant that features a favorite color, or start with a favorite flower that has grown well for you in the past. Build around that plant by adding others that complement it and thrive in similar conditions. As you choose, include different flower sizes as well as different foliage colors and textures. Also keep in mind the thriller-filler-spiller guideline.

USE THE COLOR WHEEL. If you are unsure about what colors go together, look at a standard color wheel. Monochromatic combinations are one option—shades of all purple or all red, for example. Analogous colors, which are next to each other on the color wheel, also can be the start of a handsome combination. Try yellows with oranges, or blues with violets, for example. Complementary colors also are eye-catching. These pairings include yellows with purples, oranges with blues, and

←
Complementary color combinations are always effective. This pot pairs two native species with flowers in complementary hues: purple asters (*Symphyotrichum* spp.) with yellow goldenrods (*Solidago* spp.). Photo by Margaret Fisher.

↑
This combination pairs hot-hued red geraniums and impatiens together with purples and blues, which are analogous colors next to each other on the color wheel. The purple flowers are petunias, while the blue ones are annual edging lobelias (*Lobelia erinus*).

Foliage combinations can be as eye-catching as ones featuring flowers. This combination features two variegated hostas: 'Inniswood', with chartreuse leaves edged in darker green, and white-edged *Hosta ventricosa* 'Variegata'. Autumn fern (*Dryopteris erythrosora*) adds texture and a coppery green hue.

reds with greens. Base your design on a color wheel combination, then select different flower sizes and foliage colors to create your design.

CHOOSE COOL OR WARM COLORS. Color temperature offers another great way to create eye-catching combinations. Cool colors, the colors of the sky and water, are blues, purples, and greens. Warm colors are the colors of the sun and warm, sunny days: reds, oranges, and yellows. Cool colors are calming and tend to recede visually, so they can make a space look larger. Warm colors are exciting and seem to pop forward. Combine different flower colors with the same or similar temperature as you mix foliage colors and textures.

KEEP FOLIAGE IN MIND. When making any combination, don't forget that leaves can be a big feature because of size, color, and texture. Green leaves are obvious, but there also are plants with variegated, chartreuse, burgundy, and purple foliage. Variegated leaves can be more than just white or yellow with green, too. Cannas can have leaves boldly striped with bright colors, and caladiums are marked with a variety of colors and patterns.

MIX AND MATCH AT THE NURSERY. To combine plants while shopping, start with one plant that appeals to you. Pick up other potential companions as you wander the nursery aisles, building a mix of colors, heights, and forms. Double-check your final selections before checking out to make sure all of your choices need the same growing conditions and will be happy in the site you have available.

FIND INSPIRATION AT HOME. Favorite pieces of fabric or rug patterns are another useful source of color inspiration. Base your selections on the color combinations you find there. You can also use the color of a favorite container or a feature of your home, such as a brightly colored door, as inspiration. Use the color wheel or color temperature to fill out your combination. Feature orange flowers in a blue container, for example.

REPEAT AND ECHO. To help unify the overall design, repeat colors or color combinations throughout the garden. In a group of containers, for example, repeating a particular color—either the same flower or two or more flowers featuring the same color—helps visually link the individual containers.

COPY, BUT ADAPT. If you fall in love with a combination from some other part of the country or the world, don't despair. Look for heat- and humidity-loving substitute plants to create your own regional version.

SET YOURSELF A CHALLENGE. Maybe you want a container with all white or all pink flowers. Foliage combinations are fun to create, too. Try an all-green one by combining plants with different leaf shapes, textures, and various shades of green. Or play off patterns. For example, combine a large hosta with white-edged leaves with a smaller one bearing leaves with white or yellow centers.

ROOM TO GROW

For combinations that last, avoid overcrowding. Eye-catching combinations overflowing with plants routinely appear in magazines and other media. Sometimes called living flower arrangements, these are stuffed with as many plants as possible to create showy, instant displays. While they may be just the ticket for dressing up a porch or deck for a special occasion, these types of arrangements tend not to last very long. Overcrowded plants are susceptible to disease, grow less vigorously, and wilt more frequently because roots and top growth don't have enough room. If you need a living flower arrangement for a special occasion, or receive

→
Repetition unifies this handsome collection of containers. Ferns, wax begonias, coleus, and a host of other plants are present, but the pots of colorful caladiums (*Caladium bicolor*) that edge the display down the steps are the element that creates a unified picture. Photo by Evelyn Watkins.

one as a gift, consider taking it apart after its big day, and use the plants in a few different containers or garden beds.

To give plants adequate room to fill in, grow roots, and thrive for months, plan on three or four plants from 4-inch pots to fill a 10- or 12-inch container. Select four to six plants for a 14-to-16-inch pot and six to eight for containers up to 20 inches. Select fewer plants if one of your choices is very vigorous or is much larger than its companions. The spacing information on the plant tag will give you an idea of the size and vigor of the plant. Giving plants room to grow means they will take a few weeks to fill in, but the plants will last much longer. One option for creating combinations that are pretty from the start is to select one larger plant to be the centerpiece of your design. Fill in around it with smaller cell-pack-size plants.

To stretch your plant-buying dollar, look carefully at each pot before you buy. Many growers create overflowing containers by planting several smaller plants in each container. Generally, they are already overcrowded. Separating and replanting them makes sense if you consider per-plant cost, plus it gives them much-needed growing room.

When you get the pot home, tip the soil ball out of the container, cut apart the root balls to separate the plants, then replant them individually. Give them a bit of TLC for a few days while they recover by keeping them in the shade and evenly moist but not wet. You can provide shade with upturned bushel baskets, burlap draped over plant stakes, or other shade coverings. The same process works for overstuffed decorative containers.

This large container accommodates about seven plants. Sage (*Salvia officinalis*), ornamental cabbage, and a red-leaved cockscomb (*Celosia argentea*) add foliage interest. An ornamental pepper and a chrysanthemum contribute spots of color.

Plants for Butterflies & Beneficials

Selecting plants that belong to specific families is an easy way to attract butterflies, pollinators, hummingbirds, and many other beneficial insects to your garden. Two plant families top the list: the aster or daisy family, Asteraceae, and the mint family, Lamiaceae. In the examples below, native species are marked with a flower ( ).

Loads of garden favorites belong to the aster family, including zinnias, dahlias, marigolds, and asters. Other family members include purple coneflowers (*Echinacea* spp.), black-eyed Susans (*Rudbeckia* spp.), goldenrods (*Solidago* spp.), Stokes' aster (*Stokesia laevis*), and gayfeathers (*Liatris* spp.).

Mint family plants include coleus (*Plectranthus scutellarioides*) and salvias or sages (*Salvia* spp.), along with herbs such as lavender, rosemary, and basil. Plants in the carrot family, Apiaceae, including dill (*Anethum graveolens*), fennel (*Foeniculum vulgare*), and parsley (*Petroselinum crispum*), are effective as well.

Also include plants that feed the larvae of butterflies and other insects. Fortunately, aster- and mint-family plants support larvae of many butterflies and other insects, so planting from these families is a good start. If there is space in your yard, oak trees (*Quercus* spp.) support more butterfly and moth larvae than any other genus. Even if you don't have space for one, advocate for planting native oaks in parks, public areas, and neighborhood gardens to support native insects.

Honeybees are the best-known pollinators that visit our gardens. A huge variety of other insects also perform this essential service, including solitary bees, bumblebees, wasps, butterflies, and moths.

If possible, include milkweeds (*Asclepias* spp.) in your garden to support monarch butterflies. Butterfly weed (*A. tuberosa*) is best known, and it can be grown in large containers in full sun in Zones 3 to 9. Of course, many other plants support native insects. There are guides on the internet that list specific butterfly species and the plants that support their larvae. Some need one specific plant for their larvae, while others use a variety of trees and perennials. Filling even small gardens and containers with a diverse selection of plants helps support pollinators.

Annuals, Perennials & Overwintering

Many plants that fill our gardens with summertime color are killed by frost at season's end. In their countries of origin, however, many are tropical perennials that simply cannot withstand freezing temperatures. In areas where they do not survive the winter, these plants are referred to as tender perennials. Provided they are protected from winter cold, tender perennials can be grown season after season. At garden centers, tender perennials are often displayed with annuals. If you are interested in overwintering, read plant and display labels—and ask questions.

The lists in this book include annuals along with both tender and hardy perennials. Exactly which plants are tender and which are hardy depends on where you live and how cold the winters are in your area. To determine your hardiness zone and average winter low temperatures, ask your local extension agent or find your garden on the US Department of Agriculture's plant hardiness zone map (https://planthardiness.ars.usda.gov). First and last frost dates plus seed sowing and transplant dates also are linked to your hardiness zone.

←

While the flowers of butterfly weed (*Asclepias tuberosa*) are popular with many pollinators, including this zebra swallowtail, *Asclepias* species are absolutely vital for monarch butterflies. They are the only plants that support monarch larvae.

↑

To feed black swallowtail butterfly larvae, include parsley-family plants in the garden. These include parsley, dill, and fennel, along with carrots and Queen Anne's lace (both *Daucus carota*).

There is no need to say goodbye to favorite tender perennials that may not survive winter cold. Cannas, such as 'Pink Sunburst', are among the plants that are easy to overwinter. Overwintering saves money and also yields bigger plants that are ready to go into the garden next season.

Some tender perennials survive outdoors north of their typical hardiness range if planted in a protected location or given a thick layer of mulch or other protection. In areas where outdoor protection is not enough, you can replace tender perennials annually or overwinter them indoors. The easiest way to overwinter is to cut back top growth and dig clumps or move containers indoors before the first fall frost. For example, cape plumbago (*Plumbago auriculata*) is an evergreen South African shrub hardy in Zones 9 and 10. North of Zone 9, cut back the plant in fall and overwinter it indoors. Like most tender perennials, it needs bright, cool (50°F–60°F) conditions and soil that is kept on the dry side throughout the winter. Move tender perennials back to the garden in spring after danger of frost has passed.

Cannas and dahlias are tender perennials that are easy to overwinter. On the border between Zones 7b and 8, leaving them in the ground and mulching heavily may be all they need. If you are solidly in Zone 8, simply leaving them unprotected in the ground over winter is fine. North of Zones 7b or 8, dig the plants after frost but before the ground freezes. Cut back the tops to 2 or 3 inches and carefully wash soil off the roots. Dry them thoroughly, and then wrap them in newspaper or paper bags. Store them in boxes or open tubs in a frost-free spot. Inspect them regularly and discard any rotted roots. Sprinkle with water if they become shriveled. Plant out after danger of frost has passed. You can start them indoors in tubs of barely moist potting medium. In spring, canna rhizomes can be divided with a gardening knife. Cut the tuberous roots of dahlias apart at the same time. Each dahlia division must have a portion of the main stem attached to the tubers in order for the clump to resprout.

Hardiness varies from species to species and even among cultivars, so check out specific recommendations for favorite plants. Bananas (*Musa* spp.) are one example. Some only survive where temperatures do not dip below 45°F, while others are hardy into the southern reaches of Zone 7. Where not hardy, they can overwinter indoors as a houseplant or in a cool (over 40°F), bright spot. To overwinter large specimens on or around the last frost date, either cut the foliage back to 6 or 8 inches and store containers in a cool spot or dig the plants, wrap the roots in plastic, and store as above. Water occasionally to keep the soil barely moist over winter.

Cuttings are another option that works for many plants, including coleus. Carry a jar of water with you when taking cuttings. Cut fairly long stems just below a leaf joint, and immediately put them in water. Fill pots with a 50-50 mix of moist vermiculite and perlite. Keep cuttings in water as much as possible during the preparation process. To prepare cuttings for rooting, recut stems to 3 or 4 inches and remove all but the top few leaves. Make a hole in each pot with a pencil, plunge the damp stem tip of each cutting into rooting hormone, stick it into the moist

Cuttings offer another way to overwinter favorite plants. Since individual cuttings are small, it saves space indoors when compared to potted plants and makes it possible to carry a favorite foliage color or flower into next summer's garden.

Indicates a native species or one of its cultivars.

Indicates a plant that attracts hummingbirds, butterflies, bees, and/or other pollinators.

medium, and firm the vermiculite mix around it. Label each cutting as you stick it. Set pots in a spot with high humidity, such as under plastic or in an old aquarium with a lid. Setting containers on a heat mat designed for seedlings speeds rooting. Keep the medium evenly moist. Check for roots after several weeks by *gently* tugging on the cutting. Move rooted cuttings into containers with moist potting mix.

Plants for Containers & Small-Space Gardens

All of the plants in the lists that follow tolerate the heat and humidity that characterize southern summers. Throughout, native species and their cultivars are marked with a flower ( ). Native plants are the best choices for supporting birds, native insects, and pollinators. Species that attract hummingbirds, butterflies, bees, or other pollinators are marked with a butterfly ( ).

EASY PLANTS FOR SUN

Use the tender perennials and annuals on this list in full or part sun. They also can grow in bright partial shade. All tolerate heat and humidity. They also withstand some drought once established, although evenly moist, well-drained soil is best. Many herbs also make great additions to sunny containers and small-space gardens. For a list, see the "Herbs" section in chapter 4.

Unless otherwise noted in the descriptions, plants are only hardy in Zones 10 and 11, meaning in South Florida and the very southern tip of Texas. (Average minimum winter temperature in Zone 10 is 30°F–35°F.). North of Zone 10 use them as annuals and replace each season, or treat them as tender perennials and overwinter using the techniques outlined above.

Flowering maple 'Orange Hot Lava', a hybrid of *Abutilon megapotamicum*, is a tender perennial that thrives in heat and blooms from early summer to frost. It will also bloom over winter as a houseplant. Its flowers are hummingbird favorites.

Abutilon spp. and hybrids. Flowering maples. Grown for their dangling, lanternlike flowers, abutilons bear maplelike leaves and either upright or pendant stems. *A. megapotamicum* and its hybrids are upright and make handsome thrillers in combinations. Flowers come in shades of red, orange, and yellow. Hardy to Zone 8, plants are shrubs in frost-free areas but grow to about 4 feet tall and wide in containers.

Alternanthera spp. Alternantheras. Two species are striking foliage plants with leaves that are brightest in full sun. Flowers are insignificant. *A. dentata*, commonly called Joseph's coat or upright calico plant, is 1 to 3 feet tall, features purple, burgundy, pink, or chartreuse leaves. 'Little Ruby' has burgundy leaves with red undersides and is 12 inches tall, spreading to 16 inches. *A. ficoidea*, also commonly called Joseph's coat and copperleaf, is 6 to 12 inches tall, spreading to 18 inches. Its green leaves are blotched with hot pink, red, cream, or other colors. For either species, pinch stems to keep plants compact. Select plants with the brightest foliage for overwintering.

Angelonia angustifolia. Summer snapdragon. Grown for its upright racemes of snapdragon-like flowers in shades of purple, lavender, red, pink, and white from spring to fall, summer snapdragon ranges from 1 to 3 feet, spreading to 2 feet. Serenita series plants are compact (to about 16 inches) and can be grown from seed. Hardy to Zone 9. 🦋

↑

While green-leaved peppers (*Capsicum annuum*) are the norm, ornamental pepper 'Purple Flash' brings brilliant foliage to the garden in shades of purple and nearly black with splashes of white. Its round black fruit is edible but extremely hot.

→

Eye-catching red Madagascar periwinkle (*Catharanthus roseus*) is the hands-down thriller in this antique container surrounded by white-edged hostas and sweet alyssum (*Lobularia maritima*).

Capsicum annuum. Pepper. Handsome in containers, ornamental peppers range from 12 to 15 inches tall and wide. Leaves are either green, mostly purple ('Black Pearl' or 'Purple Flash'), or marked with purple, cream, and green. All feature showy fruit ripening to shades of red, orange, black, or greenish white. Plants are easy from seed, and small ones can be dug in fall for overwintering.

Catharanthus roseus (formerly *Vinca rosea*). Madagascar periwinkle, annual vinca. Showy and long blooming, this popular plant bears flat-faced, five-petaled flowers from early summer to frost in shades of pale to dark pink, red, white, and purplish pink. Blooms often feature an eye with a contrasting color. Plants are 6 to 18 inches tall and spread as far. Well-drained soil is best.

Celosia argentea. Cockscomb. Typically grown as annuals, cockscomb plants bear flower clusters in three different forms: plumelike with either a wide (plumosa) or narrow (spicata) base or densely crested (cristata) like a rooster's comb. Flowers, which can be cut and hung to dry, come in shades of red, burgundy, pink, orange, and yellow. Leaves are green or tinged with purple or maroon. Height varies from 1 foot to 4 feet or more. Select compact cultivars for containers. Deadhead the flowers as their color fades. Stems are brittle, so handle with care. Some selections can be grown from seed, and plants can be propagated from cuttings. 🦋

Cockscomb (*Celosia argentea*) comes in fiery colors such as red, yellow, orange, purple, and pink. This collection of hot-colored blooms includes orange coneflowers and hot pink zinnias.

Centaurea cineraria and *Jacobaea maritima* (formerly *Senecio cineraria*). Dusty miller, silver ragwort. Both of these daisy-family species feature deeply cut white, silver, or gray-green leaves covered with dense hairs that bring a handsome, feltlike texture to combinations. Gardeners typically remove the cream-to-yellow flowers. Plants are 6 inches to 2 feet tall, spreading to 12 inches. *C. cineraria* is hardy to Zone 8; *J. maritima* to Zone 7. Take cuttings in fall or dig plants to overwinter.

Chrysanthemum spp. Hardy garden mums. These autumn garden favorites come in shades from yellow, orange, and red to pink, purple, and white. Flowers can be single or fully double. To add color to fall gardens, use mums as specimens or in combinations. Typically, mums are treated as annuals and tossed once they stop blooming, but they can be grown as perennials. Give plants at least 6 hours of full sun and well-drained, evenly moist soil. Check soil moisture daily by sticking a finger into the top inch of soil. If it is dry, water. If it is moist, wait and check again the next day. For longest bloom when buying mums look for plants that have buds but few open flowers. Zones 5 to 9. 🦋

White-foliaged dusty miller (*Centaurea cineraria* or *Jacobaea maritima*) accents the larger pot in this pairing. On the left, black-eyed Susan vine (*Thunbergia alata*), underplanted with lantana, climbs an antique garden tuteur. The right-hand container features purple-and-silver-leaved inch plant (*Tradescantia zebrina*), plus pink geraniums and grassleaf spurge (*Euphorbia graminea*).

Chrysanthemums are perfect plants for adding a spot of color to a container or small-space garden in fall. Orange and yellow are two of the many colors available. Here, the chartreuse foliage of ornamental sweet potatoes (*Ipomoea batatas*) spills out between plants.

Cosmos spp. These annual daisy-family plants feature showy flowers from early summer to frost. Both are easy from seed sown where the plants are to grow just before the last frost. *C. sulphureus* comes in hot colors, including orange, yellow, and red. *C. bipinnatus* 🌸 bears blooms in shades of pink, red, and white. Height varies from 1 or 2 feet to 6 feet, and plants spread to about 3 feet. Choose newer dwarf forms for containers. Drier, poorer soil is best, as rich, moist conditions promote taller plants and flopping. Deadhead spent blooms or cut back taller plants to promote more flowers. 🦋

Cuphea ignea and *C. × hybrida*. Cigar flower, firecracker plant. An abundance of small, tubular red or orange flowers tipped in white make these tender perennial shrubs excellent fillers in containers. Plants bloom from spring to frost and are 1½ to 2½ feet tall and wide. Pinch stem tips to promote branching and denser or less leggy growth. 🦋

Dichondra argentea. 🌸 Silver ponysfoot, silver nickel vine. Native to the southwestern United States, this is a trailing vine that makes a handsome spiller. Plants are quite drought tolerant and need well-drained soil. 'Silver Falls' features silvery, rounded, fan-shaped leaves. Flowers are insignificant. Plants are 2 to 4 inches tall but can trail 3 to 6 feet in a single season.

Euphorbia graminea. Grassleaf spurge. Much like perennial baby's breath, grassleaf spurge produces mounds of airy white flowers from spring to frost above narrow green leaves. Several cultivars are available, including 'Inneuphdia', sold as Diamond Frost, and 'Glitz'. Diamond Frost features extended bloom because plants are sterile and do not produce seeds. Plants are about 14 inches tall and wide. Cut them back periodically to encourage branching, compact growth, and more flowers.

Gaillardia spp. Blanket flowers. *G. pulchella* 🌸 is a tough, drought-tolerant native annual ranging from 1 to 1½ feet and spreading to 1 foot. Plants bear red-and-yellow daisylike blooms with darker

In this pretty combination, dwarf pink cosmos (*Cosmos bipinnatus*), orange marigolds, and yellow lantana stand out against a backdrop of dark red coleus.

centers from early summer to frost. *G.* × *grandiflora*, a short-lived perennial hybrid, has yellow, orange, or red daisylike flowers with a maroon or orange band on each petal. 'Mesa' is a cultivar developed specifically for sun in the South. In the Deep South, plant in fall for winter-to-spring and early summer bloom.

Ipomoea batatas. Sweet potato. This morning glory relative is grown as a root vegetable for its fleshy edible tubers or as an ornamental for its handsome foliage. Ornamental sweet potatoes feature long vines of heart-shaped or lobed leaves that are chartreuse, purple, or variegated. They rarely flower. Tubers on ornamental types, while edible, are not as tasty as food-garden types. The vigorous, 6-to-12-inch-tall plants can spread to 10 feet in a season. Control them by pinching and/or pruning. Hardy to Zone 9, they can be overwintered by taking cuttings or digging and storing the tubers.

Ornamental sweet potatoes (*Ipomoea batatas*) are handsome, vigorous plants that can easily overwhelm less vigorous neighbors. They make wonderful spillers, but be prepared to prune to keep them in check. Here, they are planted with evergreens, Dragon Wing series begonias, and white-flowered impatiens.

Lantana camara. Lantana. Grown for their rounded, 1-to-2-inch clusters of colorful, red, pink, yellow, or white flowers, lantanas typically are hardy from Zone 9 south, although a few cultivars are hardy into Zone 7. Avoid planting this species in frost-free areas, where it is a problematic invasive plant. In addition, leaves and berries are toxic to humans, cats, dogs, horses, and other ungulates. In areas where plants are not hardy, look for compact cultivars such as 'Bandana' and 'Bandito', both about 1 to 2 feet tall and wide.

Pelargonium spp. Geraniums. Best-known zonal geraniums (*P.* × *hortorum*) bear large showy, rounded flower clusters in shades of pink, red, orange, purple, and white atop handsome, rounded leaves. Plants range from 1 to 3 feet tall and wide. Ivy geraniums (*P. peltatum*) have smaller flowers and trailing stems that make them excellent choices for hanging baskets or for use as spillers in containers. Scented geraniums also are available and effective for adding fragrant foliage to the garden. All geraniums have trouble tolerating heat and humidity, so give them a spot with about 4 hours of sun and afternoon shade the rest of the day. Look for new heat-tolerant zonal geraniums. Soggy soil causes root rot, so give plants rich, well-drained soil. Deadhead spent flowers and pinch stems to encourage branching and busy growth. Overwinter by moving plants to a bright, cool spot or take cuttings.

Pentas lanceolata. Egyptian star flower. Grown for its showy 4-inch clusters of small, star-shaped flowers, pentas bloom from summer to frost in shades of pale to dark pink, magenta, lilac, or sometimes white. Plants generally are 1 to 2 feet tall and wide, although they can reach 3 to 6 feet in frost-free areas.

Petunia hybrids. The showy saucer- or trumpet-shaped blooms of petunias come in all colors except brown and true black. While petunias can be grown from seed, newer hybrids, including popular Supertunias, only are propagated by cuttings. Plants range from 9 to 12 inches tall. Depending on the selection, they can spread to 3 feet. Pinch stems at planting time, deadhead flowers to keep plants blooming, and cut

↑

Egyptian star flower (*Pentas lanceo-lata*) blooms best in full sun but also tolerates light shade. Here, its pink flowers, which attract hummingbirds, are combined with variegated plectranthus (*Plectranthus* 'Athens Gold') and a dark-red-leaved coleus.

→

Purple-and-yellow petunias make a surprising, pinwheel-like feature in this concrete container. Pale-yellow-and-white petunias fill the rest of the container.

stems back when plants get leggy. If plants decline in midsummer, cut back stems to renew plants for fall bloom. Plants require evenly moist soil. Avoid drought and wet conditions. 🦋

Salvia spp. Salvias, sages. This huge genus in the mint family includes many excellent plants for containers and small-space gardens. Salvias bear erect clusters of two-lipped flowers, some with showy bracts at their base, in shades of red, pink, lavender-blue, and purple. For containers and small-space gardens, compact selections are generally best, including Texas sage (*S. coccinea* ✿), mealycup sage (*S. farinacea* ✿), and autumn sage (*S. greggii* ✿). All are hardy to Zone 8; *S. greggii* to Zone 7. Scarlet sage (*S. splendens*), from South America, is a tried and true garden performer hardy to Zone 10. Read labels for specifics on height and spread. All can be overwintered. 🦋

This grouping of containers features fan flowers (*Scaevola aemula*) as spillers in the front pot. Behind them are summer snapdragons (*Angelonia angustifolia*) in purple as well as lavender. The petunia-like purple blooms are Mexican petunias (*Ruellia simplex*) just beginning to flower. The purple foliage of inch plant (*Tradescantia zebrina*) echoes the flowers and helps unify the display.

More Easy Plants for Sun

Evolvulus glomeratus. Dwarf morning glory. Blue flowers early summer to frost. Non-vining.

Helianthus annuus. Sunflower. Large, daisy-shaped flowers in summer. For a small garden buy compact or dwarf cultivars. Start sunflowers from seed or plants.

Helichrysum italicum ssp. *serotinum*. Curry plant. Feathery, silver-gray foliage features curry-scented fragrance but not flavor.

Tradescantia spp. Tradescantias. Two trailing selections make handsome spillers: T. *pallida* 'Purpurea' (sometimes listed as *Setcreasea purpurea*), purple heart, bears violet-purple leaves. T. *zebrina*, inch plant, is hardy to Zone 8 and features leaves variously striped in green, white, pink, chartreuse, and purple. Cuttings root in water or rooting medium.

Scaevola aemula. Fan flower. This Australian native is an 8-to-18-inch-tall spiller that spreads to about 2 feet. Plants bear a wealth of fan-shaped, lavender, purple, pink, or white flowers from summer to frost. They thrive in heat and tolerate drought.

Tagetes spp. Marigolds. A familiar sight in sunny gardens everywhere, these daisy-family plants typically are grown as annuals. They bear single, semidouble, or double flowers in shades of yellow, orange, and maroon. Flower size varies, generally from 2 to 5 inches, depending on the type. Most common garden selections reach 1 foot in height and spread as far. African or American marigolds can reach 4 feet and spread to 2 feet. Remove spent blooms to keep new ones forming. Buy plants each year or start from seed.

Verbena × *hybrida*. Garden verbena. *Verbena* is a large genus that contains both hardy and tender perennials. Garden verbenas are popular, short-lived tender perennials. (The "× *hybrida*" connotation indicates they are the result of crosses among various species and cultivars.) They produce rounded 3-inch clusters of small, tubular flowers from

Cool-Season Flowers

Flowers that bloom in wintertime are a bonus for southern gardeners. Here are a few for adding color to containers and small-space plots. Plant in fall and replace them once hot weather returns. All attract butterflies, bees, and other pollinators.

Antirrhinum majus. Snapdragon. In Zones 7 to 10, expect flowers anytime the temperature remains above freezing. 🦋

Aurinia saxatilis. Basket-of-gold. Expect flowers from late winter into spring. 🦋

Brachyscome iberidifolia. Swan River daisy. Expect flowers from late winter into spring. 🦋

Lobularia maritima. Sweet alyssum. Plants bloom in winter in frost-free areas or in early spring farther north. 🦋

Viola spp. Pansies and violets. Pansies (*V.* × *wittrockiana*), Johnny-jump-ups (*V. tricolor*), and horned pansy or horned violet (*V. cornuta*), also referred to as violas, are all excellent cool-season choices. Plant in fall for bloom from winter to early summer, when hot weather returns. 🦋

Foliage plants also add garden interest through the winter months. Ornamental cabbage and kale (*Brassica oleracea*) are colorful from fall until winter weather cuts them down, while parsley (*Petroselinum crispum*) adds foliage during cold months that is both pretty and useful.

late spring to fall in shades of pink, rose, red, violet, blue, purple, yellow, and white. Plants, which make handsome trailers, range from 9 to 18 inches tall and spread from 1 to 2 feet. Remove spent flowers to keep plants blooming, and pinch stems to encourage branching and dense growth. Cut plants back if growth slows in hot weather to encourage new growth. Replace plants annually or, north of Zone 9, take cuttings or dig plants in fall to overwinter indoors. 🦋

Zinnia spp. Zinnias. These popular annuals come in a vast array of shapes and sizes. Height ranges from 6 inches to 4 feet, spread from 6 to 18 inches. Blooms range from single 1½-inch daisies to double 3- or 4-inch blooms. They come in solid colors and bicolors in shades of pink, orange, red, yellow, peach, and white. Zinnias are available as plants, but they are easy from seed, which offers the widest range of colors and sizes. For best results, read descriptions on labels or seed packets. Look for forms developed to withstand heat and humidity. Sow seeds where the plants are to grow, or start them indoors and transplant after danger of frost has passed. For extended bloom, sow a few seeds every two weeks until early summer. Pinch to encourage branching, and remove flowers as they fade. 🦋

Zinnias have much to recommend them. Not only do they bloom for a long season, are easy to grow from seeds, and come in a huge array of colors, shapes, and heights, but they also are favored by butterflies and other vital pollinators. Photo by Susan Bennett.

EASY PLANTS FOR SHADE

The plants on this list appreciate a spot that receives some amount of shade—morning sun and afternoon shade, dappled shade, or bright daylong shade. Few plants survive in full shade that lasts all day, such as a spot under evergreens. Heat also can be a factor in finding the best spot, and sites that receive morning sun and afternoon shade are better than ones that receive morning shade and afternoon sun, when daytime temperatures are highest.

All the plants listed below prefer evenly moist, well-drained soil, although most withstand some drought once they are established. Unless otherwise noted in the descriptions, plants are only hardy in Zones 10 and 11. North of Zone 10 use them as annuals and replace each season or treat them as tender perennials and overwinter using the techniques outlined above.

> *Begonia* spp. Begonias. Colorful and easy to grow, begonias are among the stars of the shade garden. Perhaps best known are wax begonias (*B. semperflorens-cultorum* group) with red, pink, or white single or double flowers from spring to frost above mounds of fleshy green, maroon, or bronze leaves. While they can withstand sun, they flower best in bright or dappled shade. Compact plants are 6 to 8 inches tall and wide; standard types reach 12 inches. Dragon Wing series begonias are especially tolerant of heat and drought, and they also bloom with more shade than wax begonias require. Hardy to Zone 8.
>
> *Browallia speciosa*. Bush violet, amethyst flower. This tender perennial produces mounds of green leaves topped by rich blue, tubular, five-lobed flowers with white centers. Plants are generally 1 to 2 feet tall and wide. Pinch stems to encourage branching and bushy growth. Keep the soil evenly moist. Hardy to Zone 9. 🦋

Indicates a native species or one of its cultivars.

Indicates a plant that attracts hummingbirds, butterflies, bees, and/or other pollinators.

Red Dragon Wing begonias add a spot of color hanging alongside a row of evergreens. While these tough begonias tolerate heat and humidity, and are satisfied with a sunny spot such as this one in spring, a location with afternoon shade will mean less watering and better performance once summer weather sets in.

Caladium bicolor. Caladium, angel wings. These tuberous tender perennials are grown for their bold, colorful, arrow-shaped leaves used as specimens or thrillers in combinations. The leaves, which tend to scorch in full sun, feature a variety of patterns that combine shades of pink, red, green, and white. Plants range from 1 to 2½ feet tall. Give them rich, evenly moist soil. Plants are hardy and tubers can be left in the ground from Zone 8 south. To overwinter in the north, bring plants in before the first frost, remove the soil and store tubers at no less than 45°F in dry peat or wood shavings. Or bring in pots and store the tubers dry in the pots. Start them indoors in early spring and transplant to containers or beds after the last frost.

Caladiums (*Caladium bicolor*) feature foliage in a wide range of colors and patterns. Here, they are combined with houseplants, including variegated-leaved begonias, spending the summer outdoors. Photo by Evelyn Watkins.

Hypoestes phyllostachya. Polka dot plant. Grown for their showy leaves, polka dot plants feature green leaves heavily blotched with either white or pink. The green may show up as blotches or simply as green veins. Many gardeners remove the insignificant flowers. Plants range from 1 to 2 feet and spread to about 1 foot. They make colorful fillers.

Impatiens spp. Impatiens. Two groups of hybrid impatiens are popular in gardens. Common impatiens or busy lizzie (*I. walleriana*) produce mounds of single or double flowers from spring to frost in shades of pink, salmon, rose, red, lilac, purple, orange, and white. Flowers can be solid colors or bicolors, and plants range from 6 inches to 2 feet tall and

Hot pink New Guinea impatiens (*Impatiens hawkeri*) share space with dark-pink-and-white wishbone flowers (*Torenia fournieri*), grassleaf spurge (*Euphorbia graminea*), and blue edging lobelia (*Lobelia erinus*).

wide. Give them a spot in part to full shade. New Guinea impatiens (*I. hawkeri*) are larger plants ranging from 9 inches to 4 feet tall, spreading to 3 feet. Flowers appear from late spring to frost and come in shades of pink, orange, salmon, red, lavender, and white. SunPatiens are New Guinea hybrids developed to tolerate more heat and humidity than other hybrids. Although recommended for full sun to part shade, in the South a spot in part shade, bright dappled shade, or morning sun and afternoon shade is best. Both species are tender perennials and widely available in spring. Most gardeners replace them annually, although they can be overwintered by digging plants or taking cuttings in early fall.

Phormium tenax. New Zealand flax. Also simply called phormiums, these tender perennials produce bold clumps of colorful, sword-shaped, grassy, or irislike foliage. Leaves may be green marked with white and/or pink as well as red-orange, bronze and green, or purple. Plants bear red blooms in summer, but container-grown specimens rarely bloom. Height varies, with compact types growing to about 2½ feet, medium ones to 4 feet, and full-size ones to 6 feet. Clumps spread to 3 feet or more. Compact or medium types are best for most containers. Phormiums make handsome specimens or can be used as flaglike thrillers. While suitable for full sun in the North, a spot with morning sun and afternoon shade or one with daylong dappled or bright shade is best in the South. Phormiums are hardy from Zone 9 south. In colder areas, they are best kept in containers, which can be sunk to the rim in garden beds and moved indoors to a cool, bright spot for overwintering.

Plectranthus scutellarioides (formerly *Solenostemon scutellarioides* and *Coleus blumei*). Coleus. The colorful leaves of coleus come in a huge array of color combinations, shapes, and sizes. Pinch stem tips to remove the insignificant flowers and encourage branching and bushy growth. Plants range from 6 inches to 3 feet or more and spread as far. Give them evenly moist soil that does not dry out and a spot in part to full shade. Some newer cultivars tolerate full sun, but a spot with some shade reduces maintenance because plants require less watering. Plants are widely available in spring, and coleus also can be started from seed. Some of the best colors and forms can only be propagated from cuttings. Save special plants by taking cuttings before frost in fall or by digging plants for overwintering.

Strobilanthes dyeranus. Persian shield. This tropical tender perennial boasts iridescent, 8-inch-long, silvery-purple leaves with dark purple edges and veining. Plants typically range from 1 to 3 feet tall, although they are taller in frost-free areas. Flowers are insignificant. Plants tolerate full sun in the North, but foliage color generally is best in partial or dappled shade. Give plants consistently moist soil. Pinch stems to encourage branching and bushy growth. Dig plants or take cuttings in fall for overwintering or to renew plants if the foliage declines on older, woody growth.

←
This tough, colorful foliage plant is best known simply as coleus, although botanists now classify it as *Plectranthus scutellarioides*. Hundreds of cultivars are available, and they are easy to overwinter as cuttings. These containers feature 'Fishnet Stockings', 'Salsa Verde', 'Golden Victorian', and an unknown red-leaved cultivar.

↓
Iridescent purple leaves with green veins are the hallmark of Persian shield (*Strobilanthes dyeranus*). White impatiens and chartreuse-leaved creeping Jenny (*Lysimachia nummularia* 'Aurea') complete this combination.

More Easy Plants for Shade

Asparagus densiflorus. Asparagus fern. Bears arching evergreen or semievergreen stems with a fernlike appearance. The roots are hardy into Zone 9. Avoid planting this invasive species in all frost-free regions.

Begonia sutherlandii. Sutherland begonia. A low-growing tuberous species bearing a profusion of orange flowers from spring to frost over bright green leaves. Plants are hardy to Zone 8. Dig to overwinter or collect the tiny bulbils that form in the leaf axils in fall.

Fuchsia × *hybrida* or *F. magellanica.* Fuchsia, lady's eardrops. Popular but difficult to grow, fuchsias prefer temperatures between 60°F and 70°F and stop flowering when daytime temperatures exceed 76°F. Look for a heat-tolerant cultivars either online or at your local nursery. Keep the soil evenly moist but not wet. 🦋

Heliotropium arborescens. Heliotrope. Best with afternoon shade or bright dappled shade in the South, heliotropes bear clusters of small, fragrant, lavender or purple flowers. 🦋

Plectranthus spp. Plectranthus. Two coleus relatives are worthy of consideration. P. 'Mona Lavender' bears showy clusters of purple flowers. P. forsteri, commonly called Swedish ivy, features fragrant green leaves edged in white or chartreuse.

Wishbone flower (*Torenia fournieri*) is a handsome tender perennial for shade or part sun. Use it as a trailer or spiller in containers, in hanging baskets, or for a spot of color in any shady garden bed. Pinch stems to encourage denser, bushier growth. Keep the soil evenly moist. Newer heat- and humidity-tolerant offerings are more tolerant of southern summers.

Torenia fournieri. Wishbone flower. Grown for their two-lipped, trumpet-shaped flowers, torenias bear showy, bicolored flowers in shades of purple, lavender, pink, deep pink, and white. Plants bloom from spring to frost and are 6 to 12 inches tall and spread as far. They require consistently moist, well-drained soil in part to full shade. Mulch the soil to keep roots cool and retain moisture. The species and older cultivars do not tolerate heat and humidity well, but new cultivars, including Wave series and Kauai Mix series plants, tolerate both. Use torenias as fillers, spillers, or specimens. Take cuttings or dig plants to overwinter. 🦋

BOLD CHOICES FOR POTS & PLOTS

⚘ Indicates a native species or one of its cultivars.

🦋 Indicates a plant that attracts hummingbirds, butterflies, bees, and/or other pollinators.

Consider these plants for large containers or as focal points in small-space gardens. Most prefer full sun to part shade. Give plants that need protection from hot afternoon sun a spot with morning sun and afternoon shade, bright dappled shade, or part shade.

Unless otherwise noted in the descriptions, these plants are only hardy in Zones 10 and 11. North of Zone 10 use them as annuals and replace them each season, or treat them as tender perennials and overwinter using the techniques outlined above.

Acalypha spp. Acalyphas. A. *hispida*, chenille plant, bears showy, drooping, fuzzy red flower clusters over a long season on 4-to-6-foot plants. Protect plants from hot afternoon sun. A. *wilkesiana*, copperleaf, is a handsome 2-to-4-foot foliage plant with colorful leaves mottled with green, purple, yellow, orange, copper, red, pink, and/or white.

Amaranthus tricolor. Joseph's coat. This is a 2-to-4-foot annual grown for its colorful foliage in shades of green, purple, yellow, red, pink, and/or copper. Start from seed annually, and give plants afternoon shade in hot climates.

Brugmansia spp. Angel's trumpets. These showy, but highly poisonous, tender perennials produce enormous, pendant, often fragrant trumpet-shaped blooms from summer to frost in white, pink, or yellow. Plants are 6 feet or more in height and hardy into Zone 8. Overwinter at 40°F with minimal watering. 🦋

Canna × *generalis*. Canna. These bold tender perennials, which grow from fleshy rhizomes, are prized for their showy, rounded clusters of red, pink, orange, white, or yellow flowers in summer as well as large, showy leaves. For maximum impact in containers and small-space gardens, choose cultivars with boldly colored or showy variegated foliage. Full-size plants reach 6 feet or more, but dwarf forms that reach about 3 feet are perhaps best for containers and smaller spaces. Most garden cannas are hybrids, but golden canna (*C. flaccida* ❀) is a wetland species native in the Southeast. It can be used in moist to wet soil in containers or gardens. Cannas are hardy from Zone 7 south. 🦋 In the northern reaches of Zone 7, give them extra mulch in fall or move container into a cool garage or other indoor space for extra protection.

Colocasia hybrids. Elephant ears. These tender perennials are grown for their huge, heart-shaped leaves that are green, purple, nearly black, or green marked with pink and/or white. Height ranges from 3 to 10 feet depending on the cultivar. Hardy from Zone 8 south, plants need part shade and rich, moist soil. They can be grown in standing water. (Add Bti granules [*Bacillus thuringiensis* ssp. *israelensis*] to the water to control mosquitoes.) Common green-leaved types produce tubers, but newer selections do not and are overwintered in pots. Keep them above 45°F and water sparingly when overwintering.

Add drama to any garden by including large plants with bold stature. This grouping includes variegated elephant ears (*Colocasia* 'White Lava') and variegated cannas (*Canna* 'Pink Sunburst') along with purple-leaved peppers (*Capsicum* 'Purple Flash').

Dahlia hybrids. Dahlias. Grown for their showy single or double flowers that come in nearly all colors, dahlias bloom in early summer, tend to slow down in the hottest months, and begin blooming again in fall. For containers and small-space gardens, look for heat-tolerant cultivars that are compact or dwarf, because full-size dahlias reach 6 feet. See "Annuals, Perennials & Overwintering" in this chapter for information on storing the tuberous roots.

Hedychium spp. Ginger lilies, garland flowers. These produce clumps of lush, tropical-looking foliage topped by showy clusters of flowers in shades of yellow, gold, orange, white, and red. Plants bloom from summer into fall, depending on the species or cultivar, and range from 3 to 6 feet or more, spreading as far. Compact (3-foot) selections are best for containers and smaller gardens. Many selections feature fragrant flowers. Give them average to wet soil. Hardiness varies from Zones 7 to 10. Give plants extra protection in Zone 7 or overwinter indoors. *Hedychium* species are not the source of culinary ginger. 🦋

Musa spp. Bananas. To add a tropical look to any garden, bananas are hard to beat. For containers and small-space gardens, look for dwarf selections such as 'Truly Tiny' or 'Super Dwarf Cavendish', both about 3 feet tall. Full-size bananas can reach 20 feet. Hardiness varies, but for most selections north of Zone 10, dig clumps before fall frost, cut them back to 6 or 8 inches, place them in a tray of barely moist builder's sand, and store in a dark, cool spot at 45°F–50°F. Or move containers indoors to a cool (above 40°F but ideally higher) spot and water sparingly. Plants can be tipped out of their pots for storage.

Plumbago auriculata. Cape Plumbago. This species features abundant clusters of true-blue flowers. Where hardy, from Zone 9 south, plants reach 15 feet, but they are easy to keep smaller with pruning. From Zone 8 north, overwinter in a cool, sunny space and water sparingly, or cut plants back hard and store in a cool dark place. 🦋

→
Bananas (*Musa* spp.) add lush, tropical appeal to the garden whether they produce fruit or simply large, tropical leaves. Here, 'Truly Tiny' is underplanted with Sutherland begonias (*Begonia sutherlandii*).

Hardy Perennials

For beautiful container and small-space combinations that last for years with minimal fuss, look no further than hardy perennials. The plants in this section can be grown outdoors year-round as far south as Zone 9. Most will struggle in summer heat in Zones 10 and 11. Plan on dividing them after a couple seasons. Share offsets or settle them elsewhere in your garden.

 Indicates a native species or one of its cultivars.

 Indicates a plant that attracts hummingbirds, butterflies, bees, and/or other pollinators.

HARDY PERENNIALS FOR SUN

While many annuals and tender perennials bloom nearly nonstop for the entire summer, hardy perennials tend to flower over a shorter season. Use the plants listed here to create a progression of color in the garden or combine them with one or more of the longer-blooming plants featured earlier in this chapter. All need a spot in full sun to part shade. Unless otherwise noted, all are hardy from Zone 9 north. None do well in the heat and humidity of a South Florida summer (Zones 10 and 11).

Purple coneflowers (*Echinacea purpurea*) are tough, easy-care perennials that bloom from early summer to midsummer. Although native to moist meadows and prairies, plants tolerate drought. Compact forms, such as 'Pica Bella', shown here, are handsome in containers.

Echinacea purpurea. Purple coneflower. This tough, drought-tolerant native bears daisylike flowers with purplish-pink petals and brownish-orange centers over a long season in summer. Height ranges from 2 to 5 feet. Cultivars in shades of pink, orange, yellow, and white are available. Deadheading extends bloom. Zones 3 to 8.

A piece of driftwood becomes the perfect home for sedums (*Sedum* spp.) and hen-and-chicks (*Sempervivum* spp.) because it provides the well-drained conditions these plants need.

Plants for Dry Soil & Sun

Tough heat- and drought-tolerant plants may be just the solution for creating stunning low-maintenance plantings. Give the plants listed here well-drained soil and full sun or part sun. Unless otherwise noted, all can be grown outdoors in Zones 6 to 9.

Succulent-leaved plants such as sedums or stonecrops are a good place to start. Low-growing, ground cover types range from 3 to 6 inches tall and feature colorful leaves plus small clusters of generally yellow, pinkish-purple, or white flowers. Taller sedums include popular showy stonecrop (*Hylotelephium spectabile*, formerly *Sedum spectabile*) and October daphne (*H. sieboldii*, formerly *S. sieboldii*). Both bear pink flowers in fall that attract butterflies and pollinators. Pick up several different sedums at your local garden center to create a combination. For more unusual choices, shop online.

Other choices for dry soil and sun include native red or coral yucca (*Hesperaloe parviflora*), which produces grasslike clumps of evergreen leaves that can reach 5 feet. Red flowers attract hummingbirds, and plants can be grown into Zone 10 as well. Houseleeks or hen-and-chicks (*Sempervivum* spp.) also make great additions to containers and dry, sunny sites. Finally, portulaca or rose moss (*Portulaca grandiflora*) is a handsome annual that thrives in dry soil and sun.

For large containers, consider one of our native yuccas: *Yucca filamentosa*, *Y. flaccida*, or *Y. gloriosa*. All produce 3-to-4-foot-tall clumps of evergreen, lance-shaped leaves and taller panicles of white flowers. Variegated forms are especially eye-catching.

For gardeners with space to overwinter plants indoors, or gardeners in Zones 9 to 11, consider *Agave* spp., *Echeveria* spp., *Manfreda* spp., or *Mangave* spp.

Fragaria virginiana. Wild strawberry. A low-growing ground cover or spiller in combinations, this species bears white flowers in spring followed by edible red fruit. Plants are 3 to 8 inches tall and spread vigorously by runners to several feet. The attractive three-part leaves turn scarlet in fall. Zones 3 to 9.

Hemerocallis spp. and hybrids. Daylilies. These popular perennials bear trumpet-shaped flowers in midsummer primarily in shades of orange, yellow, red, pink, and nearly white. Each flower lasts for only one day. For containers and small-space gardens, compact, reblooming cultivars are especially effective. Look for gold 'Stella de Oro' or yellow 'Happy Returns', both about 1½ feet tall when in bloom. Keep the soil evenly moist to encourage repeat bloom. Hummingbirds and some bumblebees visit the flowers. Zones 3 to 9.

Hibiscus moscheutos. Hardy hibiscus, swamp rose mallow. Grown for its huge, 4-to-9-inch flowers in shades of pink, magenta, deep red, and white, this is a species for large containers or in-ground plots. Plants bloom from midsummer to early fall, and each flower lasts only one day. Height ranges from 3 to 7 feet in height, spreading to 4 feet. Look for compact cultivars (about 4 feet tall) that suit smaller gardens, and pinch stems when they are 8 and then 10 inches long to encourage branching and bushy growth. 'Luna Red' and 'Luna White' are 2 to 3 feet tall. All are heat tolerant and thrive in average or very wet soil. Zones 5 to 9.

Commonly called hardy hibiscus or swamp rose mallow (*Hibiscus moscheutos*), this native species thrives in very wet soil as well as rich, ordinary garden loam. Compact forms, such as 'Luna White', shown here, are best for containers.

Penstemon digitalis. Foxglove beardtongue. This species bears panicles of white flowers from late spring to midsummer. Plants range from 1½ to 3 feet and tolerate a wide range of soils. 'Husker Red' features white flowers and burgundy leaves. 'Dark Towers' and 'Blackbeard' bear pink flowers and very dark burgundy foliage. The foliage is semievergreen in southern zones. Zones 3 to 8.

Foxglove beardtongue (*Penstemon digitalis*) is popular with pollinators and makes a handsome addition to containers and any sunny garden. In this combination, dark-purple-leaved 'Dark Towers' shares space with another native, Mexican feathergrass (*Nassella tenuissima*).

Phlox spp. Phlox. Garden phlox (*P. paniculata* ✿) bears rounded clusters of showy, often very fragrant flowers in summer. Plants range from 2 to 4 feet and spread to 3 feet. For containers and small spaces, look for compact cultivars that stay between 2 and 3 feet tall, and also look for resistance to powdery mildew. 'David' is an outstanding white-flowered form. Creeping or moss phlox (*P. subulata* ✿) is a 4-to-6-inch evergreen spiller. Plants bloom in spring in shades of pink, white, or lavender. Phlox are best in dappled shade in the South. Zones 4 to 8. 🦋

Rudbeckia fulgida var. *sullivantii*. Orange coneflower. By far the best-known representative of this species is the cultivar 'Goldsturm', grown for its orange, daisylike flowers with dark centers. Plants are 2 to 3 feet tall, spreading to about 2 feet. They bloom from early summer to early fall. Deadheading keeps plants flowering. Zones 3 to 9.

Solidago spp. Goldenrods. These native plants bloom from summer to fall and are among the best perennials for supporting native insects. They are not responsible for causing hay fever. Wreath goldenrod (*S. caesia*) is 1 to 4 feet tall. 'Golden Fleece', a compact cultivar of autumn goldenrod (*S. sphacelata*), ranges from 15 to 18 inches tall and blooms for several weeks in fall. Both species thrive in sun or partial shade. Zones 4 to 8.

Stokesia laevis. Stokes' aster. This clump-forming perennial produces showy lavender-blue or white flowers from spring to midsummer that resemble large cornflowers or bachelor's buttons. Individual flowers are 2½ inches across and are carried above clumps of evergreen leaves. Plants are 1 to 2 feet tall, spreading to 1½ feet. Give them well-drained soil, especially in winter. Zones 5 to 9.

Verbena canadensis (also listed as *Glandularia canadensis*). Rose verbena. A native wildflower throughout the Southeast, rose verbena is a short-lived perennial that self-sows if conditions suit. Plants are 8 to 18 inches tall, spreading to 2 feet, and bear rounded clusters of rose-pink to pinkish-purple flowers from spring to fall. Deadhead spent flowers and pinch stems to keep growth compact. 'Homestead Purple' is a popular cultivar with purple blooms. Zones 4 to 9.

Indicates a native species or one of its cultivars.

Indicates a plant that attracts hummingbirds, butterflies, bees, and/or other pollinators.

HARDY PERENNIALS FOR SHADE

Foliage reigns supreme in shade gardens. To create eye-catching foliage combinations, choose plants with leaves that feature different colors, sizes, shapes, or textures. For example, in a large container with a bold, variegated hosta, add a maroon-leaved heuchera and an evergreen fern to ensure a colorful combination even without accompanying flowers.

Unless otherwise noted, all the plants listed below are fine from Zone 9 north. None do well in the heat and humidity of a South Florida summer (Zones 10 and 11). Many of the perennials listed here flower as well, and you can also combine them with the annuals and tender perennials listed under "Easy Plants for Shade" earlier in this chapter.

Asarum spp. Wild gingers. These are low-growing perennials with handsome heart-shaped, often variegated, evergreen leaves. Flowers are borne under the foliage and not readily visible, but they do attract pollinators. Species native to the Southeast, also listed as *Hexastylis* spp., include A. *arifolium*, A. *harperi*, and A. *minus*. Handsome A. *splendens* is from China. Zones 5 to 9. Canada wild ginger (A. *canadense*), best in Zones 4 to 6, is not as tolerant of southern heat and humidity.

Aspidistra elatior. Aspidistra, cast iron plant. The common name of this species celebrates its nearly indestructible nature. Plants grow to 3 feet and spread to 2 feet or more. North of Zone 8, grow aspidistras in large containers and move them indoors to a frost-free area over winter. The species has green leaves (flowers are insignificant), but invest in a variegated cultivar such as white-striped 'Variegata' to add interest to foliage combinations.

Epimedium spp. Epimediums, barrenworts. These spring-blooming perennials thrive in shade and tolerate drought once established. The leathery leaves are compound with leaflets that mostly have heart-shaped bases and pointed tips. Many are evergreen, and there are forms that feature colorful foliage. Cut the leaves to the ground in midwinter. Otherwise, the early spring flowers will be hidden under last year's foliage. The small blooms are borne in loose clusters and come in shades of yellow, pink, orange, purple, and white. Depending on the species, height ranges from 6 to 18 inches, and with time plants spread to 1 or 2 feet. Most epimediums are hardy in Zones 5 to 9.

Ferns. These shade-loving perennials add wonderful texture to any shade combination. See "Ferns for Texture in Shade," below, for a list of native and non-native ferns that will make excellent additions to a shady spot.

Hedera spp. Ivies. Although English ivy (*H. helix*) and Algerian ivy (*H. canariensis*) are popular, both are vigorous spreaders that have been declared invasive in many areas. Both quickly and relentlessly climb trees and spread across gardens. Variegated forms are less invasive than the all-green species, but it is best not to plant them. English ivy is hardy in Zones 4 to 10, Algerian in Zones 7 to 10.

Heuchera hybrids. ✿ Heucheras. Grown primarily for their evergreen foliage, heuchera hybrids produce mounds of rounded to heart-shaped lobed leaves. Leaves come in shades of chartreuse, silver green, purple, and maroon, and they are often marked with prominent veins in a contrasting color. Plants generally range from 6 to 12 inches, but some cultivars reach 18 inches. Sprays of tiny flowers appear in summer. Hybrid heucheras are best in Zones 4 to 8, and they struggle with heat. Sites that do not receive any full sun are best in the South. Some cultivars are more heat tolerant, including 'Citronelle', 'Caramel', and 'Red Lightning'.

Heucheras (*Heuchera* hybrids) are versatile shade plants equally at home in containers or shady beds and borders. They make striking specimens, as illustrated by these pots of heuchera 'Magma' decorating the steps leading from a patio.

Hostas make handsome additions to shade gardens and containers alike. For eye-catching combinations, look for unusual cultivars. There are selections with textured as well as variegated leaves, and plants come in all sizes. 'Cathedral Windows', shown here, is just one of the hosta cultivars that tolerate southern heat and humidity.

Hosta spp. Hostas. These perennial favorites are grown primarily for their mounding clumps of handsome foliage. Plants come in all sizes, from diminutive selections that top out at 2 inches, to giants that can reach 3 feet tall and spread to several feet. Leaves come in shades of green, chartreuse, blue green, and gray green. Cultivars with variegated leaves may be marked with yellow, white, blue green, and more. Summer-borne white or purple bell- or trumpet-shaped flowers are carried in loose racemes. Use hostas alone as specimens or combine them with heucheras, ferns, or other perennials. Typically, hostas are recommended in Zones 3 to 8, but cultivars that are fine in Zone 9 are available, so look for them at reputable garden centers locally or for lists online. 🦋

Lamium maculatum. Spotted deadnettle. Despite the unappealing common name, this low-growing ground cover or spiller features white, pink, or purple-pink flowers in early summer. Green leaves are marked with a center white stripe or blotch. Zones 3 to 8. Avoid extremely invasive yellow archangel (*L. galeobdolon*). 🦋

Polygonatum spp. Solomon's seals. The arching, featherlike stems of Solomon's seals feature rounded leaflets that are green or variegated with cream or white. Foliage turns yellow in fall. Plants bear small, white, bell-shaped or tubular flowers in leaf axils in spring. Fragrant Solomon's seal (*P. odoratum* 'Variegatum') is found from Europe to Japan. Small Solomon's seal (*P. biflorum* ✿) is native. Zones 3 to 8. ♥

Saxifraga stolonifera. Strawberry geranium. A mounding 6-to-18-inch-tall species, strawberry geranium spreads by stolons that root whenever they land on a suitable site. Plants produce heart-to-kidney-shaped green leaves with white veining. Loose panicles of small, white flowers appear in late spring or early summer. 'Tricolor' features leaved edged in pink. Use it as a spiller, ground cover, or specimen in a special container. Zones 6 to 10.

Tiarella cordifolia. ✿ Foamflower.
A woodland wildflower that blooms in late spring or early summer, foamflower produces 9-to-12-inch-tall mounds of heart-shaped, lobed leaves that are semi-evergreen to evergreen. Plants spread by stolons to form 1- or 2-foot-wide clumps. Small flowers are carried in loose, upright racemes. Use foamflowers as spillers in containers or in shady beds. They need evenly moist soil in summer but well-drained soil in winter. Zones 4 to 9. ♥

Foamflowers or tiarellas (*Tiarella cordifolia*) are another woodland native that are handsome in both containers and in-ground gardens. Both clumping and spreading types are available. Spreading forms can be used as spillers in container combinations. Foamflowers are handsome either alone or, as here, combined with hostas and a sedge (*Carex* spp.).

More Plants for Small Gardens

The wealth of plants suitable for containers and small-space gardens is seemingly endless. In addition to plants for sun and plants for shade, here are a few more groups to consider.

FERNS FOR TEXTURE IN SHADE

Indispensable for adding elegance to shade gardens, ferns can be used as specimens in larger containers or combined with shade-loving plants such as heucheras and hostas. In combinations, their feathery, arching leaves add contrast both in texture and form.

The list below includes some of the most heat-tolerant hardy ferns. All thrive in part to full shade. Give them evenly moist, well-drained soil. Some tolerate dry soil once established.

Cyrtomium falcatum. Japanese holly fern. Evergreen species reaching 1 to 2 feet tall, spreading to 3 feet. Good soil drainage is important in winter. Zones 6 to 10.

Dryopteris australis. Dixie wood fern. Semievergreen, natural sterile hybrid, 3 to 5 feet tall. Tolerates wet soil plus dry shade once established. Zones 5 to 9.

Dryopteris ludoviciana. Southern wood fern. Semievergreen to evergreen fern ranging from 3 to 4 feet tall, spreading to 3 feet. Zones 6 to 10.

Dryopteris sieboldii. Siebold's wood fern. Evergreen fern ranging from 1 to 3 feet and spreading as far. Established plants tolerate drought. Zones 6 to 9.

Osmundastrum cinnamomeum  (formerly *Osmunda cinnamomea*). Cinnamon fern. A 1-to-3-foot-tall species spreading to 3 feet. Best in wet to evenly moist conditions. Zones 6 to 9.

Polystichum acrostichoides.  Christmas fern. Evergreen fern ranging from 1 to 2 feet tall and wide. Needs good soil drainage and tolerates dry soil once established. Zones 3 to 9.

Nonhardy tropical ferns are suitable throughout the Southeast. In Zones 10 and 11, they can be grown outdoors all year. From Zone 9 north, overwinter them indoors in a cool, bright spot, then move them back outside when danger of frost has passed. Native macho or giant sword fern (*Nephrolepis biserrata* ) and Kimberly queen fern (N. *obliterata*) are two especially showy species that are tougher and a bit more adaptable than their popular relative Boston fern (N. *exaltata*).

 Indicates a native species or one of its cultivars.

 Indicates a plant that attracts hummingbirds, butterflies, bees, and/or other pollinators.

GRASSY FOLIAGE FOR FLAIR

Ornamental grasses and sedges (*Carex* spp.) bear graceful, arching leaves that add elegance to container and small-space combinations. Here are a few plants that fit nicely into small-space and container gardens. Unless otherwise noted, the plants listed here are perennial throughout the Southeast but best from Zone 9 north.

Carex spp. Sedges. Sedges all prefer shade to part shade and thrive in evenly moist to wet soil. The ones listed here range from 1 to 1½ feet and spread to about 2 feet. Two native green-leaved species are seersucker sedge (*C. plantaginea* ) and Cherokee sedge (*C. cherokeensis* ). Both are fine in average or evenly moist soil. Seersucker sedge tolerates dry soil. Variegated selections include variegated Japanese sedge (*C. morrowii* 'Variegata') and Evergold striped weeping sedge (*C. oshimensis* 'Evergold').

→
This striking container features a flaglike clump of Mexican feathergrass (*Nassella tenuissima*) underplanted with purple-and-silver-leaved inch plant (*Tradescantia zebrina*). The combination is especially striking because the grass echoes the chartreuse leaves of the hostas that surround the container.

Hakonechloa macra 'Aureola'. Variegated Japanese forest grass. Forms a 1-to-1½-foot mound of arching green-and-yellow leaves. Best in part shade and evenly moist soil.

Pennisetum setaceum 'Fireworks'. Purple fountain grass. While the species is an invasive self-seeder, 3-to-4-foot-tall 'Fireworks' does not produce viable seed and does not spread. Plants bear leaves marked with burgundy, pink, and green. Full sun to part shade. North of Zone 10 replace plants annually or dig and overwinter indoors.

Schizachyrium scoparium.  Little bluestem. Upright 3-to-4-foot clumping grass with blue-green leaves tipped in red. Good fall color. Prefers sun to part sun and tolerates poor, dry soil.

Indicates a native species or one of its cultivars.

 Indicates a plant that attracts hummingbirds, butterflies, bees, and/or other pollinators.

SHRUBS FOR SPECIMENS

Nearly any size plant will work as a specimen, provided it has outstanding form, color, or texture throughout the year. Use specimen plants to create a focal point, draw the eye to a particular garden feature, or highlight a stunning container. Many of the plants described earlier in this chapter make suitable specimens, but also consider handsome shrubs and small trees. These include common boxwood (*Buxus sempervirens*), croton (*Codiaeum variegatum*), cycads (*Cycas revoluta* and *Dioon edule*), dwarf junipers (*Juniperus* spp.), and palms. Depending on the plant, you can mulch or underplant with a ground cover. Topiaries also make great specimens.

Flowering shrubs to consider include gardenias (consider *Gardenia* 'Frostproof' where they are marginally hardy), hibiscus (*Hibiscus rosa-sinensis* ), and roses,  especially heat-tolerant ground cover roses such as Drift series plants.

VINES FOR HEIGHT

Use vines to decorate a trellis or create a living privacy screen, or train them up and over a deck or patio to add shade to a sitting area. In some areas, vines are trained over old awning frameworks to provide summer-time shade. Here are some flowering vines to consider.

Bougainvillea spp. Bougainvilleas. Vigorous, thorny, tropical vines, bougainvilleas need heat and full sun to produce flowers, which come in shades of red, pink, yellow, white, and purple. Full-size plants can reach 40 feet, but dwarf and compact cultivars range from 3 to 5 feet and are suitable for containers and small gardens. 'Helen Johnson' is one popular dwarf form. Zones 9 to 11.

Clematis spp. Clematis. These popular vines bear white, pink, red, lavender, blue, or purple flowers that range from 1 to 8 inches. Many are fine for large containers. Look for heat-tolerant selections, and site plants with their roots in the shade and tops in the sun. Bloom season, hardiness, and pruning requirements vary, depending on the species and cultivar.

Ipomoea spp. Morning glories. Annual morning glories bear showy trumpets in purple-blue as well as red, pink, and white. They are easy to grow from seed but can self-sow with abandon and are difficult to control. Red-flowered cypress vine (I. *quamoclit*) and cardinal climber (I. × *multifida*), both annuals, are easy from seed and attract humming-birds. Moonflower (I. *alba*) is a tender perennial with large white blooms that open at night. It is invasive where hardy (Zone 10 south), but can be grown as an annual elsewhere. Plants can be overwintered by cuttings, or container-grown specimens can be moved indoors.

Lonicera sempervirens. Coral or trumpet honeysuckle. Bears red, trumpet-shaped flowers that are not fragrant on plants ranging from 8 to 20 feet. Foliage is evergreen to semievergreen. Prune immediately after flowering. Zones 4 to 9.

Mandevilla spp. Mandevillas. These tropical vines thrive in heat, and bear 3-to-6-inch trumpets in shades of pink, red, and white. Give them rich, well-drained soil and full sun to partial shade. Pinch stems to encourage branching. Replace annually or overwinter plants in a cool, bright spot. Water sparingly in winter. Zones 10 and 11.

Maurandya scandens. Snapdragon vine, chickabiddy. Produces tubular, two-lipped flowers in shades of purple, lavender, pink, or white on 6-to-9-foot plants. Can be overwintered in the north or started annually from seed. Part shade is best in hot climates. Zones 9 and 10.

Passiflora incarnata. Passion flower. This fast-growing vine, hardy in Zones 5 to 9, bears showy, fringed, blue-and-white flowers that are 1 to 3 inches across. Fruit is edible. Plants are woody in the South and die to the ground in the North. Other tropical passion flower species are suitable as well.

Rhodochiton atrosanguineus. Purple bell vine. A tender perennial best grown as an annual, this species produces pendant, bell-shaped, mauve-pink flowers from summer to fall in sun or part shade. Typically grown from seed. Zones 10 and 11.

Thunbergia alata. Black-eyed Susan vine. A tender perennial, this species bears flat-faced orange, yellow, or white flowers with dark centers from summer to fall. Bloom sometimes slows in summertime heat. Afternoon shade is best. Easy to grow as an annual from purchased plants or seeds. Or take cuttings to overwinter. Zones 10 and 11.

An old ladder and the wooden post at the end of a fence provide support for a pretty, pink-flowered mandevilla vine (*Mandevilla* spp.). Photo by Susan Bennett.

Clumps of Spanish bluebells (*Hyacinthoides hispanica*) provide welcome spring color to this street-side container garden.

BULBS

Gardeners faced with limited space typically look for plants with long bloom seasons and handsome foliage. While few bulbs are prized for their long bloom seasons, they add color and character to the garden. Here are some suggestions on bulbs to try and ways to use them. In the discussion that follows, "bulb" refers to plants that grow from true bulbs (onions, for example) as well as corms (crocuses and gladioli), tubers and tuberous roots (dahlias and some begonias), and fleshy rhizomes (cannas). All of the following bulbs attract butterflies, bees, and other pollinators to the garden, and many feed hummingbirds as well.

BULBS FOR EARLY SPRING. Crocuses, narcissus or daffodils, and other spring bulbs are planted in fall, then emerge and add precious early color in spring. After flowering, their foliage feeds the bulb that produces next year's flowers. The yellowing leaves can be in the way when you are making room for summer-blooming plants. One option is to treat bulbs as annuals by discarding and replacing them. Or plant bulbs around the edges of the container or small plot, and reserve the center for summer flowers—or vice versa, with bulbs in the center and summer flowers around the edge. Another option is to plant them in containers that can be sunk into the soil, then lifted after flowering. Either replant them elsewhere so the leaves can finish ripening or share them with a friend. Bulbs require a certain number of hours between 32°F and 45°F in order to break dormancy and flower. Be sure to look for species and cultivars recommended for your hardiness zone.

Woodland crocus (*Crocus tommasinianus*) with lavender-purple flowers is squirrel-proof and recommended for southern gardens in Zones 3 to 8. When selecting daffodils or narcissus (*Narcissus* spp.) north of Zone 8, most are fine in southern gardens. In warmer climates, look for early-blooming types that have small flowers. Types with clusters of flowers also tend to be suitable. Species tulips (especially *Tulipa clusiana*, *T. fosteriana*, *T. greigii*, and *T. kaufmanniana* for Zones 3 to 8) fare better as perennials in the South than Dutch tulips. Pre-cooled bulbs, whose chilling requirements have already been fulfilled, also are available.

Also consider spring starflower (*Ipheion uniflorum*, Zones 5 to 9), which has fragrant white-to-purple flowers. Purple-flowered grape hyacinth (*Muscari neglectum*, Zones 4 to 9) is another good choice. For late spring to early summer blooms, consider summer snowflake (*Leucojum aestivum*, Zones 4 to 8), with white flowers, and Portuguese squill (*Scilla peruviana*, Zones 7 to 10), with softball-size lavender flower clusters. Johnson's hardy amaryllis (*Hippeastrum × johnsonii*, Zones 7 to 10) bears clusters of red trumpets.

BULBS FOR SUMMER. Cannas, dahlias, and caladiums, covered earlier in this chapter, are all ideal plants for southern summers. Tuberoses (*Polianthes tuberosa*, Zones 7 to 10) are perhaps the most fragrant summer bulbs. Plant rhizomes in spring after danger of frost has passed for bloom in summer into fall. Plants can be started in containers in early spring. To overwinter, let the foliage die back and store the rhizomes in dry peat or vermiculite.

Achimenes (*Achimenes* spp.) grow from scaly rhizomes and bear tubular, flat-faced flowers from summer to fall primarily in shades of red, pink, and purple. They are easiest kept in containers. Give them part shade. Plants are hardy in Zones 10 and 11, but farther north, simply dry off the soil and store the containers in a warm (50°F–70°F), dry spot. Resume watering the following spring.

Other summer-blooming bulbs for the southeast include crocosmias (*Crocosmia* spp., Zones 6 to 10), with red, yellow, or orange trumpet-shaped flowers; Byzantine gladiolus (*Gladiolus communis* ssp. *byzantinus*, Zones 7 to 10), with magenta, maroon, or coppery red flowers; ornamental onions (*Allium* spp., Zones 4 to 9), with round clusters of purple or white

flowers; and agapanthus (*Agapanthus* spp., Zones 7 to 11 🦋), with trumpet-shaped flowers in clusters of lavender and purple. Crinums (*Crinum* spp., Zones 7 to 10 🦋) are traditional southern favorites that are large, long-lived plants bearing showy clusters of pink, white, or red flowers in summer. They can be grown in the ground where hardy or kept in containers. Finally, rain lilies (*Zephyranthes* spp., Zones 10 and 11 🦋) are easy in pots and bear grassy leaves and funnel-shaped pink or white flowers in summer. To overwinter the bulbs, store them nearly dry in their pots in a cool spot.

Achimenes (*Achimenes* spp.), which are related to African violets and other gesneriads, grow from scaly rhizomes and are excellent bulbs for summertime containers and hanging baskets in shade. Many cultivars are available. This is pink-flowered 'Peach Blossom' shown with caladium 'Pink Splash' and a strawberry geranium (*Saxifraga stolonifera* 'Hope's Wine').

CHAPTER 4

FOOD

Growing Vegetables, Herbs & Fruit

←

Even a small food garden offers plenty of opportunities to try out new crops and techniques, including constructing homemade supports for vining crops such as pole beans.

Whether you are an experienced gardener or a beginning one, when starting a new garden it pays to keep things simple. Starting small has equal value. A small, well-managed vegetable garden can teach volumes about how to grow food, without many of the headaches a big garden brings. Even if a larger garden is in your future, build on the lessons taught by a small one. Even if your plan is to stay small, you will find plenty of opportunity to experiment with new crops and techniques every season.

Getting Started with Vegetables

Many basic gardening principles remain the same whether you are growing food or flowers. For example, all great gardens start off with good soil preparation, and compost is a valuable addition to any soil. However, managing a vegetable garden is akin to mounting a military campaign. First off, instead of looking for plants that thrive in the spot where you want to garden, know that vegetables want what they want. Your job is to find sites that make them happy. Also, to produce a harvest at the end of the campaign, you need to figure out growing schedules and get plants in the garden at the right time.

You will find information on evaluating and selecting a site, improving soil, and preparing garden beds in chapter 2. Keep in mind there's

The key to a successful food garden lies in finding sites to make your vegetables and herbs happy. Whether you grow in containers, raised beds, or the ground, for most that means sun and good, well-drained soil. Here, spring lettuce, interplanted with marigolds and still-small tomato plants, grows adjacent to a strawberry bed.

no rule that says your plants have to all be in the same spot. Depending on what works in your yard, for example, you can create several tiny plots for vegetables and herbs, plus add containers to the mix. This approach is especially helpful when finding spots that give plants exactly the conditions they require to flourish.

To produce a good-size harvest, preseason planning is a must—especially in a small garden. That means selecting crops and figuring out sowing and/or transplant dates. It also helps to develop an overall schedule for when crops go into the garden and when they will be ready for harvest. Local insight is a good place to start. Talk to local gardeners, your extension agent, or the staff at well-stocked garden centers. Find out about their favorite crops and which ones have been most successful. Also ask when they plant cool-season crops such as lettuce and broccoli and warm-season crops such as beans, tomatoes, and peppers. Local gardeners also may have surplus seedlings to share. Many state extension service websites contain invaluable information. Vendors at farmers' markets also often have transplants for sale that are suitable to your local area. Finally, you can also look for information online, but make sure you are consulting *local* sources. Sowing and transplanting dates for Virginia do not apply to Gulf Coast states, for example.

A container filled with handsome food plants—in this case cabbage and parsley—makes an eye-catching combination almost too pretty to pick.

There are options if you want a vegetable garden that is pretty as well as productive. Interplant vegetables with flowers, especially edible ones, for example. Vegetables arranged in drifts instead of conventional rows make a garden more attractive, too. Underplanting—surrounding tomatoes with basil or bush beans, for example—also helps. Or edge a vegetable plot with low-growing flowers such as marigolds. Keep in mind that vegetables can be pretty, too. Peppers and pole beans are particularly attractive, for example, as are lettuce and mesclun mixes. Herbs such as chives and rosemary also can make a vegetable garden more ornamental. Fruit crops such as strawberries can be used as edgings, and even dwarf fruit trees can be used as specimens in the garden. Finally, consider a trellis or other structure to add decorative appeal.

DECIDING WHAT TO GROW

If you are going to purchase all your plants, scout local nurseries to find out what they will offer and when plants will be available. You can also order transplants by mail. If you are planning to grow at least some plants from seed, you will need seed-starting supplies. Use the suggestions here to help sort through the options.

GROW VEGETABLES YOU LOVE. If you love salads, consider crops such as lettuce or mesclun mixes, especially the cut-and-come-again types that you can harvest over a long season. If you love spicy food, look for unusual peppers that are hard to find locally. If space is a major limitation, look for compact cultivars of cabbages or other cole crops to use space efficiently. Or try patio-type tomatoes, which are far smaller than typical ones. Be sure to ask family members what produce they love as well!

To create beds that are pretty and productive, consider edging with flowers. Here, nasturtiums, which also feature edible flowers and foliage, edge a bed of heirloom 'Toscano' kale.

START WITH EASY CROPS. Ask friends and neighbors for their thoughts on what crops are the easiest to grow. Radishes and green beans usually are near the top of every gardener's list. Other easy crops to consider include cucumbers, summer squash and zucchini, garlic, leaf lettuce, spinach, snap peas, Swiss chard, and kale. Tomatoes can be a bit more of a challenge, but compact hybrids are easy for small gardens, in part because they need less caging or trellising than full-size ones.

CONSIDER THE UNUSUAL. Vegetables that feature an unusual shape or a fun color, or ones that are expensive locally, can be great garden additions. Most are as easy to grow as conventional selections and not generally available at the grocery store. For example, buy seed for a mix of radishes or beets in different colors and shapes, grow yellow snap beans instead of green, or plant seed for round zucchini or yellow pattypan summer squash. 'Barese' is a compact, white-stemmed Swiss chard that is handsome and easy in containers. There are hundreds of types of tomatoes. Consider planting yellow ones or popular grape tomatoes. Heirloom crops are fun, too. Tomatoes 'Arkansas Traveler' and 'Black Krim' are just two heirlooms that are more heat tolerant than most tomatoes.

↑
Uncommon but thriving bedfellows are the result of this gardener's plan to accommodate several much-loved food plants. In this raised-bed garden, an onion crop, underplanted with a ground covering of strawberries, grows next to blueberries and other plants.

↓
Sun, evenly moist soil, and a structure for climbing are the key to making cucumbers an easy crop to grow. Photo by Susan Bennett.

LOOK FOR LITTLE. For space-starved gardeners, vegetables developed specifically for their compact size may be the perfect solution for fitting more plants into limited space. Look for cultivars offered as dwarf, compact, or patio-size as well as non-vining or bush forms of crops such as beans and squash. Many, but not all, are suitable for containers. Read descriptions to check size at maturity, flavor, and whether they will tolerate heat and humidity at least as well as full-size offerings. If you have space to install a trellis, growing upward saves valuable space as well. In addition to pole beans, melons are easy to trellis. Use slings cut from old T-shirts to support the fruit.

ADJUST YOUR TIMELINE. Cool-season crops such as radishes, beets, cabbage, broccoli, spinach, kale, collards, mesclun, peas, and lettuce are typically grown in spring and/or in fall up north. Throughout much of the South, though, they are grown as winter crops. To grow cool-weather crops in winter, start seeds in late summer or fall for harvest from winter to very early spring. Killing temperatures vary by crop. While heat-loving tomatoes and basil are killed when temperatures dip to 32°F, many of the cool-season crops listed above will survive into the 30s and even 20s, depending on the crop and the cultivar. Ask for recommendations locally, or search online using a phrase such as "temperatures for winter crops." If you are on the borderline for a particular crop, or if you are located in the Upper South or other areas that are a bit cooler, consider using row covers or plastic grow tunnels to help cool-weather crops through the coldest spells. To spread out the harvest and as extra insurance against unexpected cold snaps, sow several small crops every few weeks in fall.

MAKE A PLANTING PLAN

Whether you are planting in containers, raised beds, or in-ground gardens, once you have an idea of the crops you want to grow, the next step is figuring out what goes where. Admittedly, since less space means fewer crops, determining what you have room for may be a painful process. You can make a plan on paper, but there also are veggie garden

Edible Flowers

To add extra color to your garden and to salads and other dishes, grow some of the edible flowers listed here. Be sure to identify plants carefully before consuming them. Use the flowers whole or gently tear them apart to use as petals.

Basil (*Ocimum basilicum*)

Chives, leeks, and garlic (*Allium* spp.)

Cornflowers (*Centaurea* spp.)

Gladioli (*Gladiolus* spp.)

Lavender (*Lavandula* spp.)

Marigolds (*Tagetes* spp.)

Mints (*Mentha* spp.)

Nasturtiums (*Tropaeolum majus*)

Oregano (*Origanum vulgare*)

Pansies and violets. Pansies (*Viola* × *wittrockiana*), Johnny-jump-ups (*V. tricolor*), horned pansy or horned violet (*V. cornuta*), and sweet violet (*V. odorata*) are all edible.

Roses (*Rosa* spp.)

Squash (*Cucurbita* spp.)

Thymes (*Thymus* spp.)

Containers for Vegetables

For smaller pots ranging from 10 to 12 inches, consider beets, lettuce, radishes, spinach, and all sorts of salad greens. Plants such as bush beans or peas, broccoli, cabbage, bush-type cucumbers, eggplant, peppers, Swiss chard, and dwarf tomatoes will do fine with one plant per 12-to-18-inch pot. If you are growing in tubs or really large pots, consider melons (especially compact types), zucchini or summer squash, watermelons, and full-size tomatoes. In the largest containers, consider planting more than one crop: Surround a broccoli plant with mesclun or leaf lettuce. Or underplant a dwarf or patio tomato with heat-tolerant, slow-to-bolt lettuce or Swiss chard.

↑
This garden features a mix of recycled and reused containers on the sunny side of a shed. All the containers are large enough to support tomatoes.

←
For gardeners growing on balconies, overall container weight is an important consideration. These eggplants are thriving in lightweight black grow bags, which are an excellent option for reducing container weight.

planning apps for phones or computers that help figure out what crops fit where. Your plan should include what to grow from spring to summer, from summer to fall, and from late summer or fall through the winter months and into spring.

To make a simple planting plan, first list the crops you want to grow on a piece of lined or graph paper, in a notebook or garden journal, on a calendar you refer to regularly, or on your phone, tablet, or computer. List each crop in the season or seasons you will be growing it. Leave room for notes, because sowing and transplanting dates will vary. You may have crops such as lettuce and beans listed in more than one season.

Next, if you are starting plants from seed, look at the recommended sowing date for each crop, which typically is listed on seed packets or on seed descriptions in catalogs or online. Most are given in terms of the last frost date, so you will need to count back from that date. See chapter 2 for information on using and determining frost dates. Make a note on when to sow each batch of seeds and whether it is to be sown indoors or directly out in the garden where the plants are to grow. You also will find recommendations on when to transplant, so make a note of those dates as well.

While you work, keep an eye out for crops that can be sown in small batches. These include radishes, beets, lettuce, mesclun mix, and bush beans. Sowing small batches of seed every two or three weeks spreads out the harvest, so you are not confronted by a huge amount of produce all at once.

Many seeds are started 6 to 8 weeks before the last frost date, so you undoubtedly will end up with a long list of seeds to sow at or around that time. The same is true of transplant dates. Sowing and transplant dates are recommendations, not hard-and-fast rules. If you have too many things to plant on a single date, need to schedule around a trip, or have other responsibilities that curtail your gardening time, spread out sowing and transplanting duties around the suggested dates. The dates given on seed packets are generally the earliest recommended dates. Warm-season crops will be just fine if planted late. Cool-season ones such as lettuce or snap peas can be planted earlier, especially if you can cover them during cold snaps.

TECHNIQUES TO BOOST YIELDS

Maximize your harvest by using the following techniques.

SUCCESSION PLANTING. Use this technique to make the most of gardening space by planting a new crop each time one is harvested. For example, follow a spring crop of mesclun or lettuce with heat-loving beans or peppers. Just pull up the first crop once plants stop producing, show signs of heat stress, or simply begin to die, and plant the next. Late in the season, replace warm-season beans and peppers with cool-weather spinach or arugula.

INTENSIVE GARDENING. Gardeners who use this technique maximize the use of every square inch of their gardens by planting in wide rows or spacing plants close together. Instead of being planted in traditional single-plant rows, plants are arranged so they will touch at maturity. Stagger spacing to create a drift or wide row. Alternate rows of three plants next to two plants, for example. Less unplanted space also cuts down on weeds.

UNDERPLANTING OR INTERCROPPING. This, too, makes the best use of precious space by filling in around slow-growing crops such as broccoli or tomatoes with fast-growing ones such as leaf lettuce, mesclun mix, radishes, beets, bush beans, or spinach. Like intensive gardening, this not only ensures a bigger harvest but also keeps the soil covered and helps with weed control.

Lettuce, which prefers cool temperatures, can be replaced by heat-loving crops such as beans, peppers, and tomatoes later in the season. To spread out the lettuce harvest, plant small batches of seeds at 2-week intervals. The flowers of violas and pansies are edible, too.

ROTATE. Even in a small garden it is possible to rotate crops. Crop rotation ensures the soil stays fertile and also helps boost yields. Even in gardens too small to allow for moving crops from one place to another each year, adding compost in spring or fall will replace nutrients depleted by heavy-feeding crops such as tomatoes. Spread compost over the soil surface, and then cover it with mulch to keep soil moist and cool. Soil-dwelling creatures will work compost down into the soil. One simple way to rotate crops is to pay attention to the amount of nutrients each demands and alternate heavy-feeding crops with ones that are either soil build-ers or light feeders. Heavy-feeding crops include tomatoes, eggplant, broccoli, beets, cabbage, lettuce, and other leafy vegetables. From one season to the next, alternate them with soil builders such as peas and beans or light feeders such as garlic, onions, peppers, potatoes, rad-ishes, sweet potatoes, Swiss chard, and turnips.

Wide rows planted with staggered plants use bed space more efficiently than conventional ones, because less area is devoted to empty space between rows. The plants here are arranged one-two-one. At maturity, they will touch to fill the entire bed.

PLAN FOR TRELLISES & CAGES

Trellises and other structures help make the most of limited space. Plan on installing supports for crops such as tomatoes and beans before moving transplants to the garden. Otherwise, it is far too easy to dam-age seedlings during installation. A wide variety of trellises and other supports are available at garden centers and online, but you also can make your own.

Full-size indeterminate tomatoes, which continue to grow taller all season, need sturdy, 8-foot-long stakes set at least 1 foot in the ground, or 10-foot lengths of ½-inch rebar, sunk up to 2 feet in the ground. Purchased plant cages are another option for crops such as peppers and

↑
Minimize damage to plants by installing stakes and other supports before planting. The tomatoes and other plants in this side-yard garden also are protected by a fence to keep animal pests at bay.

→
Purchased or homemade supports are equally serviceable for supporting vining crops such as snap peas. Always check on the height of each crop before selecting and installing supports.

smaller tomatoes. Large, robust cages are best for full-size tomatoes. Look online for directions on making your own from concrete-reinforcing mesh. Tie stems to stakes or cages during the season with strips of old T-shirts or other soft cloth.

Tepees made of bamboo or garden stakes are an option for beans, snap peas, cucumbers, and other climbing crops. You can tie the stakes together at the top or purchase specially designed connectors. If space is available, erect two, and place another pole across the top from one to another. Add strings across the bottom from one tepee to the other and from the top pole to the string at the bottom. Place transplants at the bottom of each vertical string. Use cotton string, so strings and vines can be cut down together and composted at season's end. Depending on the situation, trellises and other supports may need wind protection or need to be attached to a fence or other support. Also, try to locate such crops on the north side of the garden so they don't cast shade on other crops.

Growing from Seed

Starting with nursery-purchased transplants is the easiest way to start a garden, but typically that means a limited selection. Growing at least some plants from seed lets you try unusual or heirloom vegetables along with a wider selection of popular hybrids. Broccoli, cabbage, okra, onions, peppers, radishes, and tomatoes are among the easiest crops to grow from seed.

To start your own vegetables or flowers from seed you will need seeds, pots, plant labels, and seed-starting mix. You also will need a window with bright light or a setup for artificial lights. A heat mat is a good investment, too, since bottom heat speeds germination. Cuttings root faster with bottom heat, too. Heat mats, available from garden suppliers, are safe and designed to work in the damp conditions under plant pots. They warm the soil to about 70°F.

For containers, buy new ones or recycle smaller (2½-to-3-inch) pots used for annuals. For best results, wash them thoroughly before reusing them. Coffee or yogurt cups or any other containers available also work, but punch a hole in the bottom to ensure adequate drainage. In general, seedlings are easier to care for if they are all in the same or similar size and type of container, because they will all need watering at similar times. Peat pots are another good option. If you use them, when you transplant tear the top edge off the pot so it doesn't emerge above the soil line. Otherwise it will wick water out of the pot creating a dry barrier that is difficult for roots to penetrate.

LIGHT FOR SEEDLINGS

Sufficient light is a must for producing stocky, healthy seedlings. Most gardeners don't have access to a greenhouse, but you can produce good-quality seedlings on a cool, but heated, sun porch (use heat mats to keep the soil warm), in a bright windowsill, or under artificial lights. Many gardeners double up light sources to ensure healthy seedlings—lights suspended over seedlings in a windowsill, for example. You can purchase lighting fixtures and stands designed especially for plants, but if you aren't sure you are going to love seed-starting (or rooting cuttings), start with ordinary shop lights suspended over your seed flats. Use chains to suspend the lights so you can adjust the height over the seedlings. The lights should be no more than 2 to 4 inches above the leaves, and chains allow you to adjust the distance as plants grow. Use a timer to turn lights on and off automatically, and give plants 14 to 16 hours of light per day.

PUTTING SEEDS TO SOIL

To sow seeds, fill pots with premoistened medium to within about ½ inch of the top. Next, sow three or four seeds per pot. To sow, press most seeds onto the soil surface and cover them with a thin layer of moistened mix—about equal to the width of the seed. When sowing tiny seeds, just press them onto the soil surface. Some seeds require light to germinate (this information will be on the seed packet). Just press these seeds onto the soil surface as well. Insert a label with the plant name and sowing date into each pot as you sow.

Most warm-season crop seedlings grow best at temperature between 60°F and 70°F, slightly cooler at night and slightly cooler for cool-season crops such as broccoli and cabbage. Temperatures that are too warm lead to taller, spindly seedlings, while cooler temperatures encourage slower growth and stockier plants that are better prospects for transplanting.

Seedlings have all the food they need to germinate in the seed itself, so once they are planted, all you need to do is keep the medium evenly moist.

CARING FOR SEEDLINGS

Once seedlings appear, continue to keep the soil evenly moist. To determine whether pots need watering, stick a finger into the soil to feel for moisture. It is fine if the surface is slightly dry as long as the soil below feels moist. Pot weight is another way to decide. Pick up a pot, then water it and lift it again to feel the difference.

The easiest way to water seeds and seedlings is to set pots in a tray of water and let the water soak up from the bottom. This prevents accidentally washing away tiny seeds and it also keeps the soil surface slightly drier, which helps prevent damping-off, a fungal disease that rots the stems just at the soil line. Or use a small bottle or other container that lets you tip water (room temperature is best) gently into each pot.

Once plants are up, feed weekly with compost tea or a diluted fertilizer solution at half the recommended strength. After three weeks, switch to full-strength. If your potting medium contains fertilizer, you do not need to feed at all.

Once seedlings have at least one true leaf, they are ready for thinning or for transplanting into individual pots. (The first leaf or leaves a seedling produces is called a seed leaf, or cotyledon. The first true leaf resembles those of the mature plant.) To thin, select the strongest seedling and simply cut off the extra ones at the soil line with scissors. This ensures the strongest seedling will have the space it needs to grow.

Soaker hoses positioned along rows of plants make watering easy and efficient.

Many gardeners sow their seeds densely and transplant seedlings to individual pots. This method requires a bit more work, but it saves space under lights. To transplant, fill new pots with moistened medium and poke a hole into the medium with a pencil or other implement. Then tip the seedlings out of their first pot and gently break apart the root ball. Handle seedlings very carefully. Pick them up by a leaf, never by the stem, because it is easy to crush or damage it. Lower each seedling into the hole so it will be at the same depth it was growing in its previous pot. Gently firm the soil around it and water.

For details on planting and moving plants to the garden, see "Plants & Scheduling" in chapter 2.

DIRECT SOWING

Some seeds are easiest and happiest if you sow them out in the garden where they are to grow. These include beans, lettuce, mesclun mix, and snap peas as well as flowers such as zinnias. To direct sow, rake the surface of your plot or container so it is smooth, then plant the seeds where you want them. Cover seeds as outlined in "Putting Seeds to Soil" above. Label each plot to keep track of what you planted and where. Otherwise, it is easy to lose track of where you need to water while seeds germinate and begin to grow.

Check plants regularly and water as necessary to keep the soil evenly moist. Thin them by cutting off surplus seedlings or pulling them up once they have several sets of true leaves. Or, if you are gentle, you can lift and replant thinnings elsewhere in the garden. Gently press down the soil around the remaining seedlings. Keep soil evenly moist until plants are well established.

Managing Maintenance

Keeping on top of weeding, watering, monitoring pests, and other problems is the best strategy for managing maintenance. Make frequent garden walk-throughs a habit, and use the information below to stay on top of problems and keep plants thriving.

WEED CONTROL 101

The best advice is to weed early and often, because weed seedlings are far easier to dispatch than full-grown ones. Keeping a layer of mulch on the soil is another first line of defense. Conventional bark mulch works, but grass clippings, weed-free straw, and chopped leaves make great mulch as well. The thickness of the layer varies. Spread up to 8 inches of coarse-textured mulches such as weed-free straw. Use no more than 4 inches for conventional bark mulch and no more than 2 inches for grass clippings or other materials that may pack down densely. Here are other useful suggestions.

WEED AFTER A RAIN. It is easier to pull up weeds roots and all if the soil is moist. If you have time to weed, but the soil is dry, water before you start pulling.

KNOW YOUR ENEMIES. While you don't need to know the names of individual weeds, it helps to know whether they are annuals or perennials. You can pull annuals, but perennials such as dandelions grow back if you don't dig the roots. Careful digging reduces weeding chores over time, because you have to deal with each plant only once and not again and again. Also, avoid tilling perennial weeds such as thistles and some grasses. Tilling chops up the rhizomes, and each piece can become a new plant. Use a thick layer of newspaper under mulch to smother them out of existence.

WINTER WEED. Some of the most common weeds sprout in late fall, grow through the winter, then flower in spring. Take time on a nice winter day to pull winter weeds when they are still small and before they set seed.

PICK THE FLOWERS. If weeds get ahead of you, at least take time to pull off flowers and dispose of them before they form seeds. This reduces the number of seedlings in the future.

ARM YOURSELF. A garden knife or a dandelion fork, also called an asparagus knife, is very effective for eliminating deep-rooted weeds. If your plot is filled with weeds that won't come up roots and all, try using a garden fork to loosen the soil to make pulling easier.

RESTORING ORDER

If your garden gets out of control with weeds and overgrown crops, don't despair. Late in the season, pull up crops that have stopped producing, and prune back ones such as tomatoes that are still going strong. Spread compost and then mulch over empty beds to get them ready for winter. A layer of newspaper, four or five sheets thick, underneath the mulch helps control weeds. Another option is to pull spent crops and plant the areas with fast-growing ones such as lettuce or radishes. Or plant cool-season crops that you can harvest through the winter such as spinach, lettuce, and kale.

In hot climates, many gardeners plan on a two-part growing season to avoid gardening during the hottest part of the summer. They grow crops from late winter through spring and early summer, let the garden go dormant, and then plant with crops to harvest from fall to winter. Especially if the first fall frost is several months away, to start the second season, pull up plants stressed by summertime heat. Replace them when you are ready to replant. For plants that just need a jump start, prune them back, spread compost alongside them, renew the mulch, and water deeply.

WATERING AND FEEDING

Vegetables typically need an inch of water per week for good growth early in the season, but by midsummer when plants are larger and temperatures hotter, the same plants may need up to 2 inches of rainfall or supplemental watering per week. The amount depends on the size of the plants, where you live, and your soil. Use a rain gauge to keep track of the rainfall your garden receives, and water when totals fall below the amount required. For more on watering and feeding, see "Caring for Your Garden" in chapter 2.

HARVESTING

Produce is the reward for all of your hard work. Whether you pick and eat right in the garden or carry your bounty to the kitchen, handle both plant and produce with care during the picking process. To reduce damage from tugging or twisting, gently hold on to the plant with one hand while you pick with the other. Careful handling keeps the plant healthy so it continues producing. You can pick with your fingers, but using scissors, garden clippers, or pruners further reduces damage to the plant.

Morning, after the dew has dried off, is the best time to pick, because the fruit will have the highest water content and be coolest then. Pick anytime on cooler or cloudy days. If a bad storm is predicted, pick tender crops such as leaf lettuce and other salad greens to prevent damage from pounding rain.

Try to pick every crop at the peak of freshness, keeping an especially close eye on crops that ripen quickly and are harder to catch at their peak. Ideally, pick snap peas and cucumbers daily. Daily picking also is best for summer squash and zucchini, which are best picked when very small and tender. Broccoli and cauliflower are best when the heads are still dense and firm. Cabbage, lettuce and other salad greens, peppers, melons, and tomatoes can be picked every few days. Finally, carrots, onions, potatoes, and winter squash can be left in the garden for a few weeks until you have time to harvest.

Pests & Other Problems

While you want to keep an eye out for insects, don't reach for a sprayer the first time you see one. Instead, watch and see what the insects are doing and try to identify them. The vast majority of insects you find are either benign or beneficial, meaning you do not need to take any steps to control them.

The techniques throughout this book are all part of the organic gardening process, which benefits people, pets, wildlife, and the environment as a whole. To find out about the biggest problems in your area and when to expect them, ask local experts, gardening friends, and neighbors what to look for and how to manage these problems organically. The following techniques will help you manage your garden organically.

ENCOURAGE BENEFICIALS. Surprisingly, the more insects active in your garden, the better, especially because beneficial species will keep the pests in check. Some beneficials attack and eat pests, while others lay their eggs on larvae that do the actual control. Planting flowers that

↑

Many wild creatures live in or visit your garden, and they depend on insects and other creatures for food. These garden helpers include species such as this pickerel frog as well as toads and other amphibians. To help support them and keep your garden in balance, before considering control measures, watch insects you see to determine if they are beneficial, benign, or pest species that are doing noticeable harm.

→

Braconid wasps are a common predator of tomato hornworms. A hornworm that has stopped eating is likely infested, whether or not the ricelike wasp pupae have emerged. Leave them so the new generation of wasps can mature and help control another generation of hornworms.

provide nectar and pollen, maintaining permanent mulched pathways, or allowing a few weeds among your vegetables and flowers are all useful ways to provide shelter and food sources for beneficials and other insects. "Bug zapper" lights are not effective at controlling pests, because they actually kill as many beneficial insects as they do pests. Birds, toads, and other garden residents also help control pests.

PLANT RESISTANT AND TOLERANT CROPS. Read seed packets and catalog descriptions to identify crops with built-in resistance or tolerance to disease(s). V stands for resistance to verticillium wilt; A for anthracnose; F for fusarium wilt; and PM for powdery mildew.

INSPECT PURCHASED TRANSPLANTS CAREFULLY. Avoid purchasing plants that appear to have insect infestations or obvious signs of disease.

HANDLE PLANTS CAREFULLY. Bruised leaves and torn stems give pests and diseases easy access to plants.

AVOID WIDESPREAD SPRAYING. The best-known beneficials are insects such as lady beetles. Widespread spraying kills them along with bees, butterflies, and beneficials such as yellow jackets, hornets, ground beetles, tachinid flies, and many true bugs that prey on caterpillars and grubs. Widespread spraying kills dragonflies, too, and they spend their days eating gnats and mosquitoes.

USE PHYSICAL AND BIOLOGICAL CONTROLS. These include blasting small pests off plants with a stream of water or using floating row covers, cutworm collars, and other barriers that keep pests away from crops. Handpicking, trapping, and pulling and destroying afflicted plants or plant parts also are effective physical controls. Bt (*Bacillus thuringiensis*) is a naturally occurring bacterium that controls various garden pests. It is available as a spray or dust and in a formulation that can be added to water to control mosquitos.

If fencing is not an option, consider using scarecrows, strings of shiny DVDs, or your own sculptures to scare away animal pests.

SPRAYS AND DUSTS. These are the last line of defense for organic gardeners and include soap sprays, horticultural oil, and other organically acceptable pesticides. Look for the word "organic" on the label. Organic sprays are less harmful to the environment than synthetic controls, in part because they biodegrade quickly.

SYMPTOMS & SOLUTIONS

Here are a few common problems to look for along with solutions.

SEEDLINGS OR SMALL PLANTS THAT HAVE FALLEN OVER OR DISAPPEARED ENTIRELY. Three main culprits cause this problem. The first is cutworms, which are fat, soil-dwelling caterpillars that chew through stems at the base or eat seedlings entirely. Use cutworm collars to control them by slipping a 2-to-3-inch-long section of paper towel or toilet paper tubing over each transplant as you move it to the garden. Press the tube into the top inch or so of soil. Or mix bran cereal with Btk (*Bacillus thuringiensis* var. *kurstaki*, available at garden centers) and spread it around all the transplants.

Damping-off causes sunken and/or soft and rotted tissue at the base of the seedling. To prevent it, before filling pots, disinfect them with a 10 percent bleach solution (one part bleach, nine parts water), use pasteurized seed-starting mix, water seedlings from the bottom, and use a small fan to circulate air. Spray seedlings with compost tea once the first true leaves emerge.

Finally, slugs and snails eat seedlings and small plants. Look for the slimy trails they leave. Organic slug bait is available, and slugs also can be controlled by homemade traps baited with stale beer.

CURLED UP OR DISTORTED LEAVES AND/OR STEM TIPS. Several pests cause this symptom, including tiny pear-shaped aphids, which are found in dense clusters and excrete sticky honeydew on leaves. Leafhoppers are wedge-shaped insects that jump and fly in all directions when startled. Spider mites create webbing in stem tips. Blast these pests off plants with a strong stream of water, attract beneficial insects for help with control, or use insecticidal soap.

YELLOW LEAF SPOTS OR GRAY, DUSTLIKE PATCHES ON LEAVES.
Many different plant diseases begin as leaf spots, and it can be difficult to identify which specific disease is infecting plants. Planting resistant or tolerant cultivars is one option. Pick or prune off afflicted leaves or growth or pull and dispose of moderately to severely infected plants. Pruning to increase air circulation around plants also is helpful.

LARGE HOLES CHEWED IN LEAVES. Various caterpillars chew holes in leaves. Handpick them and drop them in soapy water or spray Bt (*Bacillus thuringiensis*) on afflicted plants.

Herbs

Most popular herbs thrive in southeastern gardens, although selecting the right site will improve your results. Use herbs alone or combine them with flowers or vegetables. Most herbs are plants for full sun, but in the Deep South late summer heat can take a toll. Look for a site that receives sun in the morning and at least light shade during the afternoon to help plants cope with heat. Consider moving container-grown specimens to part shade during the hottest part of the summer.

Good soil preparation is essential, too, although most herbs do not require rich soil. In fact, very rich soil leads to foliage that is less fragrant and flavorful. Many prefer dry to average soil conditions and abhor wet soil in winter. Lavender, rosemary, sage, and thymes are especially susceptible, both in winter and in summer. Mints and lemon balm do need soil that remains slightly moist. Along with basil, they also prefer afternoon shade in hot climates.

Soil that holds plenty of moisture but also lets excess water drain away quickly is ideal. The standard recipe for mixing soil for raised beds (given in chapter 2) is fine. Loose soil structure is essential. Avoid walking on soil, which crushes the large pore spaces that allow water to drain away. To increase the amount of water soil holds, without creating the soggy conditions that rot roots, add additional coarse compost or

Fencing & Beyond

A fence is the best defense for larger pests such as rabbits, groundhogs, and deer. If fencing isn't an option, consider using deterrent sprays or erect wire cages around vulnerable plants. Scare tactics work, especially if you move the items around frequently. For example, try suspending used CDs, aluminum pie pans, or other shiny materials that will move in the breeze above planting beds. Rubber snakes, owl decoys, bird-scaring balloons, and scarecrows also can help control animal pests. Use floating row covers or lightweight plastic netting to keep birds away from crops.

Fencing is the most effective control for deer and other creatures. This garden is fenced with wire mesh attached to a wood fence. Photo by Susan Bennett.

←

Rosemary (*Salvia rosmarinus,* formerly *Rosmarinus officinalis*), like many herbs, makes a handsome addition to any sunny garden. This container collection also features salvia 'Rose Marvel', which adds a splash of color.

↓

Mints need evenly moist soil to grow at their best, and plants also prefer afternoon shade in hot climates. They are notorious spreaders, and keeping them in containers provides efficient control.

Seasonal Switches

For cool-season herbs, consider a seasonal switch if you garden in the Deep South. Parsley, cilantro, chamomile, and dill can be planted in fall and grown through the winter months there. French tarragon (*Artemisia dracunculus* 'Sativa'), hardy in Zones 5 to 8, also can be grown as a cool-season annual in hot climates. Farther north, these plants can be grown under row covers or tunnels over the winter or from late winter to early summer and again from fall into early winter.

Garlic (*Allium sativum*) is a perennial best planted in late summer or fall and grown through the winter in Zones 4 to 9. Remove flower stalks when they appear—chop them up and use them as you would garlic cloves. Harvest in summer when the foliage begins to yellow.

fine pine bark and replenish it annually. Also consider using coir fiber, not peat moss, which has an acidic pH. Many gardeners add perlite to improve drainage.

With all herbs, let the soil dry out somewhat between watering. Raised beds are ideal because they drain more efficiently than in-ground gardens. Taller beds—10 to 12 inches or more—drain more efficiently than shallower ones.

To maintain even soil temperatures, discourage weeds, and retain soil moisture, mulch herbs with compost or pine straw. Finely chopped bark mulch works, too. Avoid shredded bark, which mats and forms an impenetrable layer. For herbs with gray leaves such as sage and lavender, or any that require dry-to-average soil, consider mulching with pea gravel, turkey grit, or other stones. As always, keep mulch from touching plant stems.

Finally, when pruning, keep in mind that it can be stressful for your plants. Harvest by pinching or cutting stems to minimize damage to roots and top growth. On evergreen perennial herbs such as rosemary and thymes, never remove more than one-third of the growth.

Indicates a native species or one of its cultivars.

Indicates a plant that attracts hummingbirds, butterflies, bees, and/or other pollinators.

HERBS FOR SMALL SPACES

Herbs that are both attractive and useful are probably the best choices for containers and small-space gardens. Here are a few to consider. All require full sun and dry-to-average, well-drained soil.

→
Consider convenience when deciding where to grow herbs— especially ones used in the kitchen. A metal table set on pavers to reduce the need to trim grass makes this herb collection easy to care for and access for harvesting.

Chives (*Allium schoenoprasum*). This onion relative bears rounded, pinkish-purple flowers in spring and grassy clumps of foliage that add mild onion flavor to many recipes. The flowers are edible as well. Give plants either full sun or part shade. Zones 4 to 8.

Lavender (*Lavandula angustifolia*). Densely packed spikes of small purple flowers appear in summer over gray-green needlelike leaves

on 2-to-3-foot plants that spread to 4 feet. Give plants shade during the afternoon in the hottest climates. Zones 5 to 8.

Oregano (*Origanum vulgare*). This is a tough, drought-tolerant herb with gray-green leaves and tiny white flowers in summer. Shear plants to prevent them from setting seed, as seedlings will not necessarily have characteristic flavorful foliage. Zones 4 to 8.

Rosemary (*Salvia rosmarinus*, formerly *Rosmarinus officinalis*). Needlelike leaves are produced on 2-to-6-foot plants that spread to 4 feet. Small, pale-blue-to-white flowers appear in midsummer. Zones 8 to 10. A few cultivars, including 'Arp', are hardy to Zone 6. Where they are not hardy, pot-grown plants are easy to move to a cool, bright place for over-wintering.

This collection of herbs, along with some summering houseplants, sits within easy access for watering and other care.

Sage (*Salvia officinalis*). This savory herb bears gray-green leaves on 2-to-2½-foot plants that spread as far. The cultivar 'Tricolor' features gray-green leaves edged in pink and white. Zones 4 to 8.

Sweet bay (*Laurus nobilis*). Also called bay laurel, this is an evergreen shrub with glossy, fragrant leaves that are used in soups and stews. Where hardy, plants range from 10 to 30 feet or more. Keep a plant in a container from Zone 7 north and overwinter it in a cool, bright spot. Give plants rich, moist, well-drained soil and full sun to part shade. Zones 8 to 10.

Thyme, common (*Thymus vulgaris*). This popular herb bears tiny, evergreen leaves on 6-to-12-inch plants that spread as far. In summer, plants bear small erect clusters of tiny, densely packed flowers in shades of pink, purple, lavender, and white. Many cultivars are available, and thymes are effective as spillers or for edging. Zones 5 to 9.

Fruit

There are fruit crops you can grow whether you garden exclusively in containers, in raised beds, or in the ground. Nearly all of them need a spot in full sun and prefer rich, well-drained soil. A site with morning sun and afternoon shade is beneficial in the hottest climates and for plants growing in containers. For this book, the focus is on fruit crops that are easier to grow and suitable for getting a start in fruit culture.

Many fruiting plants are shrubs or trees, and small-space gardeners may only have room for one or two plants. It is possible to restrict size to some extent with regular pruning and training. Routine pruning of trees can help keep size manageable, and removing one or two old branches from shrubs annually helps renew most plants and ensure a good, continued harvest. Espaliering—growing plants essentially in two dimensions—is another option. Plants can be trained against a fence or wall or down the center of a garden bed. Training an espalier

← A variety of citrus trees, including this kumquat, can be grown throughout the Southeast. Where they are not hardy, keep citrus in containers so plants are easy to move indoors into a bright, frost-free place for overwintering. Photo courtesy of Houston Botanic Garden.

↓

With a sturdy trellis and regular training, grapes may fit into a small-space garden. Consider growing them on wires or other supports set in front of walls or fences. Or use them on trellises to create privacy. Photo courtesy of Houston Botanic Garden.

takes patience and know-how, but it is a technique any determined gardener can tackle. Fortunately, there also are compact cultivars of many popular fruit crops, both hardy and tropical. Look for dwarf cultivars of blueberries (*Vaccinium* spp.), fig (*Ficus carica*), and avocado (*Persea americana*), for example. If you want to grow bananas, look for a cultivar grown because it produces fruit; bananas sold as ornamentals may or may not flower and fruit.

Grafted specimens of typical tree fruits such as apples and peaches are available in dwarf, semidwarf, and larger sizes. Grafted trees take fewer years to bear fruit than ones grown on their own roots, and the particular rootstock used also may provide essential protection against soilborne diseases. Different rootstocks are recommended for different parts of the country, because growing conditions and disease problems differ. If you do decide to plant a fruit tree, look for a rootstock recommended for your area. Also be prepared to spray to control pests and diseases. Otherwise, it is difficult to keep plants healthy and productive.

Grapes are another crop that may not fit into a small-space garden. All types require a sturdy trellis and annual pruning once established. Muscadine grapes (*Vitis rotundifolia*) are a native southern specialty. For most cultivars, you need to plant both male and female plants, but there are self-fertile cultivars, which help save space. Hardiness varies by cultivar, as does fruit color, but muscadines can be grown from Zone 6 to 10. There also are American-type grapes developed by crossing several native species to produce plants cultivated for their berries and that feature disease resistance.

HERBACEOUS FRUIT CROPS

Herbaceous plants, meaning plants that do not have any woody branches above ground, are among the easiest fruits to add to the garden.

Cantaloupes, honeydews, melons, and watermelons are easy-to-grow crops that thrive in heat and sun. If you plant standard-size selections, plan on training them on a trellis or the south-facing side of a fence. Use slings made from old T-shirts to support the fruits and tie them to supports. Bush-type plants are an option for small spaces. The smallest ones are only 3 or 4 feet across. You can plant them in larger containers or raised and in-ground beds. Or plant them atop an old compost pile. The fruit of all these crops often rot when left in contact with the soil. T-shirt slings are one option for prevention, or consider suspending fruit in mesh bags (the type used for onions), setting them on boards, or purchasing melon cradles.

Strawberries can be grown as perennials or annuals. Either way, they need full sun and rich, well-drained soil. Plant them in raised or in-ground beds or in containers, or use a strawberry jar or tower, either one you construct yourself or purchase from a garden supplier. As with many fruit crops, the best cultivars depend on where you live, so look for local recommendations. For best results, start with new, certified disease-free plants instead of plants offered by a friend or neighbor. To grow strawberries as annuals, plant in fall, harvest the following spring or early summer, and then pull up the plants and replace them the following fall. There are several systems for growing them as perennials. One option is in wide rows. After planting, for the first year pick off all of the flowers so the plant's energy goes into root production. Cultivate around the new plants frequently. Space out runners that form so each new plant will have room to grow. Mulch with weed-free straw over winter. Harvest begins the following spring. You will need netting or a cover—hardware cloth on a frame is one option—to keep birds, squirrels, and other hungry pests at bay.

Ground or husk cherries (*Physalis pruinosa*) are related to tomatoes and peppers, and they bear sweet fruit with a flavor that resembles a cherry tomato crossed with a pineapple. The fruit is borne in a husk that turns brown when fruit is ripe. Sow seeds to start ground cherries in your garden. After the first year, self-sown plants will pop up on their own.

Strawberries are among the easiest fruits to grow in a small garden, especially in raised or in-ground beds. Strawberry towers make ideal containers, because they accommodate the maximum amount of plants in a limited space. Photo by Susan Bennett.

Indicates a native species or one of its cultivars.

Indicates a plant that attracts hummingbirds, butterflies, bees, and/or other pollinators.

EASY FRUIT CROPS

A wide variety of fruit-bearing plants, both hardy and not, make fine container plants. That is especially true if you have a place to overwinter tropical crops. Citrus (*Citrus* spp. ) crops such as Meyer lemons, blood oranges, calamondins, and Key limes are grown outside year-round in Zones 9 to 11. (Damage occurs if temperatures dip below 32°F.) North of Zone 9, all make great container subjects that simply need a cool, bright spot for overwintering. Water sparingly in winter when plants are growing slowly. Pomegranate (*Punica granatum*) is a shrub or small tree that also makes a fine container specimen. The species is hardy in Zones 8 to 10, but 'Russian 26' is hardy into the southern portion of Zone 6.

Blueberries (*Vaccinium* spp.) are among the easiest fruits to grow in the Southeast. They are handsome landscape shrubs that feature spring flowers, stunning fall foliage, and evergreen leaves. Consider using them as an informal hedge or combined in other shrub plantings. Birds are the main pest. If you don't want to share, use netting, cages, or other techniques to keep them at bay. All blueberries require full sun and moist, well-drained, acid soil that is rich in organic matter. Plants range from dwarf 2- or 3-foot tall selections to 12- or 15-foot plants, depending on the cultivar. Dwarf types are suitable for containers. While many cultivars are self-fertile, planting at least two different cultivars of blueberries that bloom at the same time improves yields and increases fruit size. Blueberries also require a certain number of chilling hours in order to bloom, and the requirements vary by cultivar. For this reason, it is important to identify selections that grow well in your area. There are cultivars for as far south as Zone 10 in Florida and ones that are hardy into New England. Highbush blueberries (*V. corymbosum*) are suitable for the Upper and Middle South, while heat-tolerant rabbiteye blueberries (*V. virgatum*) are suitable farther south into the Gulf Coast. Southern high-bush types are the result of crosses between highbush blueberries and species native to Florida. These have made blueberries an excellent crop throughout Zone 10.

Blackberries and raspberries also can be easy to grow in the Southeast. In the landscape, think of using them along the south-facing side of a fence or wall. Essentially, they form a hedgelike planting that requires wires or a trellis to keep canes upright and make harvesting easier.

All blackberries and raspberries produce canes that live for two years. Most first-year canes, called primocanes, produce only leaves. Two-year-old canes, called floricanes, bear flowers and fruit. Everbearing types produce fruit on both primocanes and floricanes. Remove floricanes after they have fruited. Choose cultivars proven in your area. Two good thornless blackberries to consider are 'Arapaho' and 'Navaho'. Both produce upright canes, which makes training and harvesting easier, and can be grown into northern Florida. Everbearing raspberries are probably the easiest choices for small-space gardeners. Here, too, look for local suggestions, since heat tolerance varies. Also, if you can plant more than one cultivar, choose ones that ripen at different times to extend the season.

There are many more fruit crops to consider. Native crops include maypop or native passion flower (*Passiflora incarnata*), a vine that is herbaceous in the north, woody farther south, and hardy in Zones 5 to 9. Elderberry (*Sambucus canadensis*) is native and also attracts beneficials. Consider it if you have a spot for a 5-to-12-foot suckering shrub that prefers medium to wet soil. Zones 3 to 9. Paw-paw (*Asimina triloba*) is a small 15-to-30-foot tree that produces fruit that tastes like bananas. Plants, hardy in Zones 5 to 9, grow in shade but need full sun to produce fruit. This species is host to zebra swallowtail butterflies.

Any book without the help of editors, copy editors, and designers is little more than a manuscript. I would also like to thank editor Cate Hodorowicz, project editor Valerie Burton, copy editor Iza Wojciechowska, and art director Lindsay Starr, plus Elaine Maisner, who got this project started.

Acknowledgments

SPECIAL THANKS TO my nongardening husband, Peter Evans, who happily supports my every gardening whim and loves the end results. I also want to thank local friends Sarah Ruckelshaus and Gayle Folger, who listened, answered questions, and provided all-around support as I wrote, experimented with plants, and took pictures for this book.

Special thanks also go to everyone who let me visit and photograph their gardens including Cynthia Saunders, Daphne Howarth, Valerie Reihl, Linda Kleinbart, Jocelyn Grover, Christina Murray, Gayle Shank, and Heather Byrne. Several others helped as well, including photographers Susan Bennett, Margaret Fisher, and Evelyn Watkins, along with Joyce Moore, who provided useful contacts, and Justin Lacy from the Houston Botanic Garden.

Any book without the help of editors, copy editors, and designers is little more than a manuscript. I would also like to thank editor Cate Hodorowicz, project editor Valerie Burton, copy editor Iza Wojciechowska, and art director Lindsay Starr, plus Elaine Maisner, who got this project started.

Index